This

Sandra Lee
semi-homemade®

grilling 2

book belongs to:

....

Special thanks to Culinary Director Jeff Parker

Meredith® Books Des Moines, Iowa

Copyright © 2008 Sandra Lee Semi-Homemade® All rights reserved. Printed in the USA.
Library of Congress Control Number 2007933386 ISBN: 978-0-696-23828-4

Brand names identified in this book are suggestions only. The owners of such brand names retain all
right, title, and interest in and to their respective brands. No manufacturers or brand
name owners have endorsed this collection or any recipe in this collection.

sem.i.home.made

adj. **1:** a stress-free solution-based formula that provides savvy shortcuts and affordable, timesaving tips for overextended do-it-yourself homemakers **2:** a quick and easy equation wherein 70% ready-made convenience products are added to 30% fresh ingredients with creative personal style, allowing homemakers to take 100% of the credit for something that looks, feels, or tastes homemade **3:** a foolproof resource for having it all—and having the time to enjoy it **4:** a method created by Sandra Lee for home, garden, crafts, beauty, food, fashion, and entertaining wherein everything looks, tastes, and feels as if it was made from scratch.

Solution-based **E**nterprise that **M**otivates, **I**nspires, and **H**elps **O**rganize and **M**anage time, while **E**nriching **M**odern life by **A**dding **D**ependable shortcuts **E**very day.

2

dedication

To the great guys and gals that make grilling
meals meaningful and memorable!

To my brothers Rich and John Paul
for marinating every day with fabulous flavor!
I am so very proud of you. —SL

Table of Contents

Chapter 1

Veggies and Sides
18

Chapter 2

Skewers
34

Chapter 3

Dogs and Sausages
50

Chapter 4

Pork and Lamb
64

Chapter 5

Things to Do with
Your Turkey Fryer
86

Letter from Sandra

Times change, but grilling is still a way to make food taste "special." Semi-Homemade® makes it simple, too, whether you're a barbecue beginner or a seasoned champ. The secret is to take savvy shortcuts where you can and make clever use of convenience products that keep the quality and taste you love, while shaving valuable minutes off the prep time. It's all possible with my unique 70/30 philosophy: mix 70% ready-made foods with 30% fresh ingredients, add a dash of creativity, and grill up a meal that's 100% fast and fabulous!

Like so many of us, I used to think of grilled food as "special food," something you did when the weekend rolled around or company came. Our old three-legged grill was the symbol of summer. Come Memorial Day, we'd dig it out, hose it down, and enjoy the fruits of its flames for three long, lazy months. My brother's lake-caught trout, my uncle's lemon-buttered flank steak, my aunt's barbecue chicken coated with sauce—these were the foods of summer, until Labor Day brought it to a bittersweet end. In college I discovered the fun of fall tailgates—beer-braised bratwurst and big, beefy burgers dripping with Wisconsin cheese. Living in California taught me that grilling is good year-round and that vegetables and fruits are as ripe for the grill as a burger or steak. Traveling taught my taste buds new spices and flavor sensations—tongue-tingling salsa, the sweet heat of curry, jerk seasoning as cool-hot as a Bahamian breeze.

Over the years, I've grilled everything from foie gras to figs, and the best recipes are here in this book—11 chapters of great grillables that are fun to cook and even more fun to share. You'll find family favorites, such as barbecue ribs, herb-roasted chicken and veggie-stuffed pork chops, paired with stepped-up sides, like Sweet Potato Salad and Grilled Asparagus with Spicy Mustard. You'll find grill-and-dip skewers for parties, smoked salads for veggie lovers, and spice-rubbed roasts for holidays. You'll even find Cajun-fried turkey, gumbo for a crowd, and a New England clambake—blackened, simmered, and steamed right in the turkey fryer.

When you want to impress without stress, there are posh dishes, like citrus-sauced lobster and wine-planked filet mignon. When you want to keep it casual, there are fish burgers, turkey burgers, hamburgers, and hot dogs—plus pizza—towering with bistro-style toppings and creative condiments. There are cool, colorful cocktails to start and warm, dreamy desserts to finish. I've even put together party menus and tablescapes that make entertaining a joy, whether you're hosting a Biker Bash or a Sunny Soiree. Best of all, every easy-to-follow recipe takes the guesswork out of grilling, giving you cook times, helpful tips, and flexible directions for grilling inside or out, any day of the week.

Where there's smoke, there's fire and something to barbecue. Grab your spatula, pour a cocktail, and let the flames begin. It's barbecue time!

Cheers to a happy, healthy life!

Sandra Lee

Tricks of the Trade

Slicing, cutting, weighting, and wrapping—learn about it all right here! For example, when you're folding snapper in banana leaves (see recipe, page 165), just wrap the sides of the leaf up to form a packet around the fish, then secure with toothpicks.

Wrapping fish in a banana leaf packet for Thai Snapper Grilled in Banana Leaves, page 165

Butterflying steak for Southwestern Stuffed Flank Steak, page 119

Removing backbone from chicken for Cuban Mojo Chicken Halves, page 143

Butterflying lamb for Spatchcooked Leg of Lamb with Tandoori Spices, page 83

All about techniques

Southwestern Stuffed Flank Steak: Butterfly the meat in this recipe by cutting it in half lengthwise, but hinged at one end. This makes it a thinner piece of meat and allows for more surface area to spread the filling.

Cuban Mojo Chicken Halves: To cut the chicken in half, cut along one side of the backbone, then cut up along the other side to remove the bone. To separate halves, cut along only one side of the breastbone.

Spatchcooked Leg of Lamb: To butterfly the boneless lamb leg, open up the meat. Split open and unroll any pieces of meat that are thicker than 1 inch.

Chicken Under Bricks: Weighting the chicken with bricks helps flatten the poultry to cook quicker. Just wrap bricks in foil and place on top of chicken.

Weighting chicken for Chicken Under Bricks, page 139

Sure, anyone can throw a hunk of meat on the grill and call themselves a master, but real grilling experts know the truth—the real magic is in the marinade.

Acidic flavors such as vinegar, wine, and citrus juice

Purchased rubs

Marinade packets

Bottled marinades

Refrigerated marinated meat

Getting started:

To make your own marinade, all you need is an acid, an oil, and any number of flavorings. The acid (which could be vinegar, wine, citrus juice, or even salsa) will soak into the top layer of the meat to help tenderize it. The oil (which could be olive, canola, vegetable, or any flavored oil) coats the meat and protects it from the heat once it's on the grill. And add flavorings for … well, flavor, of course! Try combos of herbs, spices, mustard, garlic, honey, and more. To make marinating easier, try using a purchased bottled product or a dry marinade packet (just add oil and an acid!). For a supereasy method, you can purchase refrigerated meat that is already marinated. Another easy way to add exceptional flavor is by rubbing meat with a mixture of herbs and spices—either purchased or homemade.

Grill-Master Gadgets

What's a great grilling experience without the nifty equipment? While some gadgets help you get the job done better, others are just for fun—like this branding iron personalized with my initials.

Check These Out!

Grilling planks: Another way to add flavor dimension to grilled food is by cooking it on wood planks over the coals. Some of the more common varieties of wood used include oak, maple, and alder. Heartier pieces of meat and fish, such as salmon and filet mignon, especially benefit from this flavorful method of grilling.

Vertical roaster: Everyone's heard of beer can chicken, but propping the chicken on just a can makes for a wobbly bird. Stabilize the chicken, while pumping it full of great flavor by using the vertical roaster.

Disposable grilling pan: Grill baskets are perfect for keeping veggies from falling through the grate, but they can be hard to scrub clean. These disposable pans do the same trick, and when you're done, just toss!

Disposable grilling pan

Grilling planks

Vertical roaster

13

Indirect

Indirect

Direct

Direct

Grilling 101

Gas grills generally come with thermometers but you can also find grill thermometers that sit right on the grate for charcoal grills. If you're feeling brave, you can test the temp with your hand by holding it several inches over the grate and count how many seconds you can keep it there comfortably (see "hand method" below).

Grill thermometer

Turkey fryer equipment

Heat Level	Temperature	Hand Method
Hot	450° F to 500° F	2 seconds or less
Medium-Hot	400° F to 450° F	3 to 4 seconds
Medium	350° F to 400° F	4 to 5 seconds

Electric turkey fryer

Direct Heat Grilling

Direct heat grilling is just that … placing meat directly over the heat source. Typically this is used for smaller pieces of food, such as steaks, chicken breasts, pork chops, and vegetables. For direct grilling on a charcoal grill, cover the charcoal grate with a layer of briquettes, then pile the briquettes into a pyramid. Add lighter fluid and light the charcoal. Let the coals burn for 25 minutes or until covered with a gray ash. Use long-handled tongs to spread coals across the grate. **Oil the cold cooking grate just before beginning to cook and then place it on the grill. Never spray the grate with cooking spray when it is over hot coals.**

Indirect Heat Grilling

Indirect grilling "bakes" food over a longer period of time, because the heat source is off to the side instead of directly under the food. This is ideal for larger cuts of meat like roasts. For indirect grilling on a gas grill, light the grill, leave one burner off, and place the food on the grate above the unlit burner. Close the grill. Use the grill knobs to control the heat. For indirect grilling on a charcoal grill, follow "Direct Heat Grilling" directions for arranging and lighting charcoal, using about 50 briquettes. When the coals are covered with gray ash, divide them in half and place them on opposite sides of the grill. Put a disposable foil drip pan between the piles. Open vents to increase temperature; close to decrease temperature.

Gas turkey fryer

Turkey Fryers

Although the food they produce is definitely worth it, turkey fryers can be dangerous to work with, so don't take any shortcuts with safety. Always operate the turkey fryer outdoors, on a flat grass, concrete, or dirt surface, and away from the house and other objects. If the fryer tips over, it can cause a fire (as well as serious burns!). Don't leave the fryer unattended while it's on and keep children and pets away from the area. Keep a fire extinguisher nearby and always wear an apron, oven mitts, and goggles. **Read the turkey fryer's instruction manual and safety directions carefully before you begin.**

Perfect Accompaniments

And now for my thoughts on perfect drink pairings for meals. We all have our favorite go-to picks, but when you want to try something new, here are some great sippers to get you started.

Red Stripe Lager

Harp Lager

Guinness Stout

Echelon Vineyard Pinot Grigio

Edna Valley Vineyard Pinot Noir

Solaris Napa Valley Zinfandel

A Little Sophistication

Wine has its place with grilled food too, especially when you want to make your meal a little more special. Here are three of the wines I serve time after time. Edna Valley Vineyard Pinot Noir is velvety smooth going down and brings out the rich flavors of Planked Filet Mignons with Portobello Mushrooms (page 112) perfectly. Solaris Napa Valley Zinfandel has a ruby red color and plummy flavors that are divine with any type of barbecued ribs, but especially complement Smoked Spareribs with Backwoods BBQ Sauce (page 79). And if you're in the mood for something on the white wine side, Echelon Vineyard Pinot Grigio is my pick. Its bright flavor really picks up the citrusy undertones of Lobster with Citrus Butter (page 170).

Bring on the Beer!

I love a mug of beer with my grilled foods, and here are three of my favorites. Red Stripe's full-bodied flavor goes perfectly with flavorful poultry like Cuban Mojo Chicken Halves (page 143), while Harp's clean crispness makes it an ideal companion to seafood like Grilled Snapper with Mango-Avocado Salsa (page 162). Guinness is a meal in itself, but tastes superb with hearty meats like BBQ Brisket with Guinness® Mop Sauce (page 127).

17

Veggies and Sides

It just takes one unusual ingredient to turn everyday standbys into memorable dishes. Expect the unexpected in this chapter—anything-but-ordinary vinaigrettes, dressings, and sauces that turn plain veggies and sides into summery scene-stealers. Sometimes it's a surprise ingredient, such as a Tex-Mex chile sauce in a Tuscan-Basil Vinaigrette. Other times, it's an old favorite tried a new way, like portobello mushrooms steeped in a port wine pesto.

The cooking techniques are as varied as the ingredients themselves—tomatoes smoked right on the grill, potatoes cooked on a baking sheet, beans simmered in a cast-iron skillet, marinated vegetables steamed in foil packets. The secret's in the sauce, so start with a bottled oil or dressing and play up the taste and texture. Sprinkle in a handful of herbs, a spoonful of Dijon, or a pinch of roasted garlic and you'll have outstanding veggies for any occasion.

The Recipes

Vivacious Vinaigrettes

Bottled vinaigrettes are great to have on hand. I always keep bottles of Olive Oil-and-Vinegar Salad Dressing (*Newman's Own®*) and a basic balsamic vinaigrette in my refrigerator. Play with the flavors of the bottled vinaigrettes by adding freshly chopped herbs, a spoonful of Dijon mustard, mashed roasted garlic, or even some mayonnaise. Check out the vinaigrettes in the recipes below to see what I mean:

* Port Wine Portobellos
* Smoked Tomato Salad
* Tuscan Veggie Packets

Potato Salad with Bacon Ranch Dressing

Prep 15 minutes **Grill** 20 minutes
Chill 1 hour **Makes** 6 servings

FOR BACON RANCH DRESSING:
½   cup real bacon pieces, *Hormel*®
¼   cup milk
¼   cup sour cream, *Knudsen*®
¼   cup mayonnaise, *Hellmann's*® or *Best Foods*®
1½ teaspoons ranch salad dressing mix, *Hidden Valley*®

FOR POTATO SALAD:
2½ pounds red potatoes, cut into ¼-inch-thick slices
      Nonstick vegetable cooking spray, *Pam*®
1   sweet onion, chopped
1   jar (4-ounce) pimientos, drained, *Dromedary*®
⅓   cup sliced olives, drained, *Early California*®
2   stalks celery, chopped
2   tablespoons finely chopped fresh parsley
      Salt
      Ground black pepper, *McCormick*®

1. For Bacon Ranch Dressing, in a medium bowl, combine bacon pieces, milk, sour cream, mayonnaise, and salad dressing mix. Cover and chill until ready to use.

2. For Potato Salad, set up grill for direct cooking over medium heat (see page 15). Oil grate when ready to start cooking. Lay potato slices on a baking sheet and spray both sides with cooking spray. Place potato slices on hot, oiled grill. Cook for 20 to 25 minutes or until fork tender, turning every 5 minutes. Remove from grill; cool.

3. Cut cooled potatoes into bite-size pieces. In a large bowl, combine potatoes, pimientos, onion, olives, celery, and parsley.

4. Using a rubber spatula, fold in Bacon Ranch Dressing until combined. Season to taste with salt and pepper. Chill 1 to 2 hours before serving.

INDOOR METHOD:
Prepare Bacon Ranch Dressing as directed. Preheat oven to 400 degrees F. Lay potatoes on a baking sheet and spray with nonstick vegetable cooking spray. Roast in oven about 30 minutes or until fork tender, turning once. Cool and prepare as directed.

Grilled Sweet Potato Salad

Prep 20 minutes   **Grill** 26 minutes
Chill 1 hour   **Makes** 6 servings

Traditional potato salad lightens up and goes tropical with good-for-you sweet potatoes made sweeter with pineapples cooked right on the grill and fired up with jalapeño peppers—all tossed in a Caribbean jerk seasoning. To really crank up the heat, leave a few seeds in the peppers.

2½	pounds sweet potatoes, peeled and cut into ¼-inch-thick slices
	Nonstick vegetable cooking spray, *Pam®*
1	tablespoon Caribbean jerk seasoning, *McCormick®*
1	can (8-ounce) pineapple slices, drained, *Dole®*
1	sweet onion, thickly sliced
2	fresh red jalapeño chile peppers, seeds and veins removed*
½	cup frozen creamy whipped topping, thawed, *Cool Whip®*
¼	cup sour cream, *Knudsen®*
2	teaspoons frozen orange juice concentrate, thawed, *Minute Maid®*

1. Set up grill for direct cooking over medium heat (see page 15). Oil grate when ready to start cooking. Place sweet potato slices on a baking sheet and spray lightly with cooking spray. Sprinkle with jerk seasoning, tossing to coat.

2. Place sweet potatoes on a hot, oiled grill. Cook for 20 to 25 minutes or until fork tender, turning every 5 minutes. Remove from grill; cool. Spray pineapple and onion lightly with cooking spray. Place on grill. Cook for 3 to 4 minutes per side. Remove from grill; cool.

3. Finely chop chile peppers. In a large bowl, combine chile peppers, whipped topping, sour cream, and orange juice concentrate.

4. Chop cooled sweet potatoes, pineapple, and onion into bite-size pieces. Add to bowl with sour cream mixture and fold to coat thoroughly. Cover with plastic wrap. Chill 1 to 2 hours. Serve cold.

*NOTE: Because chile peppers contain volatile oils that can burn your skin and eyes, avoid direct contact with them as much as possible. When working with chile peppers, wear plastic or rubber gloves. If your bare hands do touch the peppers, wash your hands and nails well with soap and warm water.

INDOOR METHOD:
Preheat oven to 350 degrees F. Prepare sweet potatoes, pineapple, and onions as directed. Place on foil-lined baking sheet. Bake in oven for 30 to 35 minutes or until sweet potatoes are fork tender, turning twice. Cool and prepare salad as directed.

Smoked Tomato Salad

Prep 15 minutes
Grill 8 minutes
Makes 6 servings

FOR PARMESAN VINAIGRETTE:
½   cup olive oil-and-vinegar salad dressing, *Newman's Own*®
¼   cup grated Parmesan cheese, *DiGiorno*®
2   teaspoons Dijon mustard, *Grey Poupon*®

FOR TOMATO SALAD:
6   medium tomatoes, cut in half
8   ounces fresh mozzarella, *Cantaré*®
15 fresh basil leaves, finely chopped

1. Soak ½ cup hickory wood chips in water for at least 1 hour. Set up grill for indirect cooking over medium heat (no direct heat source under tomatoes; see page 15). Oil grate when ready to start cooking. For Parmesan Vinaigrette, in a medium bowl, whisk together salad dressing, Parmesan cheese, and mustard.

2. For Tomato Salad, drain wood chips. Add to smoke box if using gas grill or place chips on hot coals if using charcoal. Sprinkle tomatoes with *salt* and *ground black pepper*. Place, cut sides up, on grill away from heat. Cover grill. Cook for 8 to 10 minutes or until skins crack and start to peel away. Remove from grill. Cool until easily handled. Peel off tomato skins. Cut tomatoes into large bite-size pieces. Tear mozzarella cheese into pieces. In a salad bowl, combine tomatoes, mozzarella cheese, and basil. Pour Parmesan Vinaigrette over salad and toss. Serve immediately.

INDOOR METHOD:
Prepare salad as directed, except do not grill or peel tomatoes. For a smoky flavor, add 1 to 2 drops liquid smoke (*Wright's*®) to the Parmesan Vinaigrette.

Tuscan Veggie Packets

Prep 15 minutes
Grill 10 minutes
Makes 6 servings

FOR TUSCAN BASIL VINAIGRETTE:
½   cup olive oil-and-vinegar dressing, *Newman's Own*®
¼   cup finely chopped fresh basil
1   tablespoon Dijon mustard, *Grey Poupon*®
1   tablespoon chili sauce, *Heinz*®
1   teaspoon Italian seasoning, *McCormick*®

FOR VEGGIE PACKETS:
1   package (8-ounce) presliced portobello mushrooms
1   package (8-ounce) baby zucchini, *Earth Exotics*®
1   package (8-ounce) baby squash, *Earth Exotics*®
1   orange bell pepper, cut into strips
½   of a red onion, slivered

1. Set up grill for direct cooking over medium heat (see page 15). Oil grate when ready to start cooking. For Tuscan Basil Vinaigrette, combine salad dressing, basil, mustard, chili sauce, and Italian seasoning. Toss Tuscan Basil Vinaigrette with mushrooms, zucchini, squash, pepper, and onion. Divide vegetables among six 12-inch-square pieces of foil. Fold together top and bottom edges of foil to seal; roll in sides of foil. Place packets on hot, oiled grill. Cook for 10 to 12 minutes or until vegetables are tender, turning once; remove. Open packets to allow steam to escape. Serve hot.

INDOOR METHOD:
Preheat oven to 400 degrees F. Prepare vinaigrette and packets as directed. Place packets on a baking sheet and bake in oven for 12 to 15 minutes or until vegetables are tender. Serve as directed.

Prosciutto-Wrapped Corn on the Cob

Prep 10 minutes
Grill 25 minutes
Makes 4 servings

4	ears of corn, shucked and cleaned
¼	cup (½ stick) butter, softened
2	teaspoons Italian seasoning, *McCormick®*
½	teaspoon crushed garlic, *Gourmet Garden®*
1	packet (3-ounce) sliced prosciutto

1. Set up grill for direct cooking over medium heat (see page 15). Oil grate when ready to start cooking. Place each ear on a 12-inch-square piece of aluminum foil.

2. In a small bowl, blend together the butter, Italian seasoning, and garlic. Spread liberally over ears of corn. Wrap corn with sliced prosciutto. Wrap in foil. Place on hot, oiled grill. Cook for 25 to 30 minutes or until corn is tender, turning frequently. Serve hot.

INDOOR METHOD:
Preheat oven to 425 degrees F. Prepare corn, wrapped in foil, as directed. Roast corn in oven for 20 to 25 minutes or until tender. Serve hot.

Asparagus with Spicy Mustard Dipping Sauce

Prep 15 minutes
Grill 8 minutes
Makes 6 servings

1	pound fresh green asparagus, trimmed
1	pound fresh white asparagus, trimmed
1	tablespoon extra-virgin olive oil, *Bertolli®*
2	teaspoons Italian salad dressing mix, *Good Seasons®*

FOR SPICY MUSTARD DIPPING SAUCE:

1	cup sour cream, *Knudsen®*
¼	cup spicy brown mustard, *Gulden's®*
1	tablespoon chopped fresh parsley
2	teaspoons lemon juice, *Minute Maid®*
1	teaspoon Italian salad dressing mix, *Good Seasons®*

1. Set up grill for direct cooking over medium heat (see page 15). Oil grate when ready to start cooking. On a large platter or baking sheet, drizzle asparagus with olive oil and sprinkle with the 2 teaspoons salad dressing mix. Toss to coat thoroughly.

2. For Spicy Mustard Dipping Sauce, in a medium bowl, combine sour cream, mustard, parsley, lemon juice, and the 1 teaspoon salad dressing mix. Cover with plastic wrap and store in the refrigerator until ready to use. Place asparagus on hot, oiled grill (can use a grilling basket, if desired). Cook for 8 to 10 minutes or until fork tender, turning often. Serve at room temperature with Spicy Mustard Dipping Sauce.

INDOOR METHOD:
Preheat oven to 400 degrees F. Prepare asparagus and Spicy Mustard Dipping Sauce as directed. Cook asparagus on a foil-lined baking sheet in oven for 8 to 10 minutes (no need to turn) or until fork tender. Serve as directed.

Port Wine Portobellos

Prep 15 minutes   **Grill** 8 minutes
Marinate 30 minutes   **Makes** 4 servings

¾	cup olive oil-and-vinegar salad dressing, *Newman's Own*®
¼	cup port wine
2	tablespoons finely chopped fresh basil
½	teaspoon crushed garlic, *Gourmet Garden*®
4	large portobello mushrooms, wiped clean and stems removed

INDOOR METHOD:

Prepare mushrooms as directed. Preheat broiler. Place mushrooms on a foil-lined baking sheet or broiler pan. Broil 6 to 8 inches from heat source for 3 to 4 minutes per side or until tender. Serve hot or at room temperature.

1. For vinaigrette, in a medium bowl, whisk together salad dressing, port, basil, and garlic; set aside. Cut mushrooms into ½-inch-thick slices and place in a large zip-top bag. Pour in vinaigrette. Squeeze air out of bag and seal. Gently massage bag to combine ingredients. Marinate in refrigerator for at least 30 minutes or for up to 4 hours.

2. Set up grill for direct cooking over medium heat (see page 15). Oil grate when ready to start cooking. Place mushrooms on hot, oiled grill. Cook for 4 to 5 minutes per side or until tender. Serve hot or at room temperature.

Smoky and Spicy Baked Beans

Prep 15 minutes
Grill 30 minutes
Makes 8 servings

Two old Southern secrets—root beer and a cast-iron skillet—turn baked beans into a sweet and smoky treat. Fry the bacon, then add the rest of the ingredients to the same skillet, baking in the flavor low and slow, campfire-style. Old-fashioned molasses makes them syrupy thick.

1	slice bacon, chopped, *Oscar Mayer*®
1	medium red onion, diced
2	cans (28 ounces each) baked beans, *Bush's*®
1	bottle (12-ounce) root beer, *A&W*®
¼	cup Worcestershire sauce, *Lea & Perrins*®
¼	cup ketchup, *Heinz*®
¼	cup yellow mustard, *French's*®
3	tablespoons molasses, *Grandma's*®
3	tablespoons chile-garlic sauce, *Lee Kum Kee*®

INDOOR METHOD:

Preheat oven to 350 degrees F. Render bacon in skillet on stovetop over medium heat. Cook other ingredients as directed. Bake in oven for 35 to 40 minutes or until beans are thickened and bubbling.

1. Set up grill for direct cooking over medium heat (see page 15). Set an 8-inch cast-iron skillet on grill to preheat. Add bacon and cook long enough to render fat. Remove bacon with a slotted spoon and place in a small bowl; set aside. Cook onion in bacon grease until soft. Return bacon to skillet. Stir in baked beans, root beer, Worcestershire sauce, ketchup, mustard, molasses, and chile-garlic sauce.

2. Cover grill. Cook about 30 minutes or until beans are thickened and bubbling. Serve hot.

Summer Vegetable Quesadillas

Prep 10 minutes
Grill 12 minutes
Makes 4 servings

1	medium zucchini, sliced lengthwise
1	medium yellow squash, sliced lengthwise
1	red bell pepper, cut into strips
1	medium sweet or red onion, sliced
1	tablespoon extra-virgin olive oil, *Bertolli*®
½	teaspoon Mexican seasoning, *McCormick*®
8	8-inch flour tortillas, *Mission*®
1	package (5-ounce) soft goat cheese, *Silver Goat*®
½	cup shredded Monterey Jack cheese, *Sargento*®
	Chunky salsa, *Ortega*®, for serving

1. Set up grill for direct cooking over medium heat (see page 15). Oil grate when ready to start cooking.

2. In a large bowl, combine zucchini, yellow squash, bell pepper, onion, olive oil, and Mexican seasoning. Place vegetables on hot, oiled grill. Cook for 3 to 4 minutes per side or until vegetables are cooked and marked. Remove from grill.

3. Spread one side of 4 of the tortillas with goat cheese. Divide vegetables among the 4 tortillas. Top with Monterey Jack cheese and remaining tortillas. Cook on grill 3 to 4 minutes per side or until cheese has melted. Serve hot with salsa.

INDOOR METHOD:
Preheat broiler. Prepare vegetables as directed. Broil vegetables on a foil-lined baking sheet 6 to 8 inches from heat source for 3 to 4 minutes. In a skillet large enough to hold tortillas, heat 1 to 2 tablespoons of vegetable oil (*Wesson*®) over medium heat. When oil is hot, carefully fry both sides of each quesadilla for 2 to 3 minutes or until golden brown, turning with a large spatula. Serve as directed.

Pizza Margherita

Prep 20 minutes
Grill 10 minutes
Makes 4 servings

For a crust both tender and crisp, stretch your dough thin and even (about ⅛-inch thickness), then grill until tiny bubbles form on top. The quality and balance of ingredients makes or breaks this pizza, so buy fresh herbs and firm, red roma tomatoes for a sunny, vine-ripened taste.

1½	teaspoons extra-virgin olive oil, *Bertolli*®
1	teaspoon crushed garlic, *Gourmet Garden*®
1	can (13.8-ounce) refrigerated pizza crust dough, *Pillsbury*®
¼	cup fresh basil leaves, finely chopped
8	ounces fresh mozzarella packed in water, thinly sliced, *Cantaré*®
3	roma tomatoes, thinly sliced
	Salt
	Ground black pepper, *McCormick*®

1. Set up grill for direct cooking over medium heat (see page 15). Oil grate when ready to start cooking. For garlic oil, in a small bowl, stir together oil and garlic; set aside.

2. Carefully remove pizza dough from can. Unroll dough and place on hot, oiled grill. Cook for 2 minutes. Using cookie sheet as a spatula, turn crust over.

3. Brush garlic oil over crust, leaving a 1-inch border. Top with 2 tablespoons of the chopped basil, the mozzarella, and tomatoes. Season with salt and pepper.

4. Cover grill. Cook for 8 to 10 minutes or until cheese is bubbly and melted. Using a baking sheet, remove pizza from grill. Top with remaining 2 tablespoons basil. Serve hot.

INDOOR METHOD:
Preheat oven to 425 degrees F. Prepared garlic oil as directed, Lightly spray baking sheet with nonstick vegetable cooking spray (*Pam*®). Unroll dough and place on baking sheet. Press out dough to 13×9-inch rectangle. Bake in oven about 7 minutes or until crust begins to brown. Brush with garlic oil and add toppings as directed. Return to oven; bake for 8 to 10 minutes more. Top with remaining 2 tablespoons basil and serve hot.

Skewers

This chapter is a tag team of two-part dishes—grill-and-go meats paired with dipping sauces to fine-tune the flavor. Lemongrass and ginger mix sweetness and sour cream to give pork and chicken Pan-Asian appeal. A barbecue-ranch dressing makes beef cowboy chic. And a silky citrus-yogurt sauce makes seafood brochettes as refreshing as a dip in the lake. Change the dip; change the dish.

Sour cream is cooking's condiment du jour, turning a ho-hum dish into one that's pleasing to the palate as well as the plate. Consider it a blank canvas, just waiting for a swish of hot sauce or a dot of jam to give it personality. If a sauce is too spicy, add a dribble of sour cream to cool the tongue. If a meat's too bland, count on sour cream and salsa to jazz it right up. So add a splash of this and a dash of that and enjoy your own culinary art.

The Recipes

Sour Cream Fix-Ups

Sour cream is like a blank canvas for flavor. If a sauce or dip is too spicy, add sour cream to cool it down. If a dish is too bland, add color and flavor by mixing a seasoning mix (*McCormick®*) with sour cream. Try the luscious dipping sauces in these artistic recipes to accompany any of your favorite grilled foods:

* Bacon-Wrapped Shrimp Skewers
* Lemongrass Chicken Skewers
* Shrimp with Green Goddess Dipping Sauce

TIP: Substitute reduced-fat sour cream to lower fat ... or give the sauce a subtle twist with low-fat options, like nonfat yogurt.

Beef Satay with Sweet Chile Dipping Sauce

Prep 25 minutes **Grill** 4 minutes
Marinate 2 hours **Makes** 4 servings

FOR BEEF SATAY:

1 ¼	pounds beef sirloin steak
1	cup lower-sodium beef broth, *Swanson*®
3	tablespoons white vinegar, *Heinz*®
3	tablespoons soy sauce, *Kikkoman*®
1	tablespoon chile-garlic sauce, *Lee Kum Kee*®

FOR SWEET CHILE DIPPING SAUCE:

1 ½	cups sugar
½	cup white vinegar, *Heinz*®
1	tablespoon salt-free Thai seasoning, *Spice Hunter*®
1	tablespoon chile-garlic sauce, *Lee Kum Kee*®
1	teaspoon salt
	Sesame seeds (optional)

1. Slice beef against the grain into ¼-inch-thick slices. Place in a large zip-top bag; set aside. For marinade, in a small bowl, combine beef broth, vinegar, soy sauce, and 1 tablespoon chile-garlic sauce. Pour into bag with beef. Squeeze air out of bag; seal. Gently massage bag to coat beef. Marinate in refrigerator for 2 hours or overnight.

2. For Sweet Chile Dipping Sauce, in a medium saucepan, combine sugar, vinegar, Thai seasoning, 1 tablespoon chile-garlic sauce, and the salt. Bring to a boil over medium-high heat; reduce heat. Simmer, stirring occasionally, for 5 to 10 minutes or until sugar dissolves. Transfer to a bowl and cool.

3. Soak 6-inch wooden skewers in water for at least 1 hour. Set up grill for direct cooking over medium-high heat (see page 15). Oil grate when ready to start cooking. Remove beef from marinade; discard marinade. Drain skewers.

4. Thread beef onto skewers. Place skewers on hot, oiled grill. Cook for 2 to 4 minutes per side or until cooked through. Remove from grill. Sprinkle with sesame seeds (optional). Serve hot with Sweet Chile Dipping Sauce.

INDOOR METHOD:
Prepare Beef Satay and Sweet Chile Dipping Sauce as directed. Preheat broiler. Place skewers on a wire rack over a foil-lined baking sheet or broiler pan. Broil 6 to 8 inches from heat source for 2 to 3 minutes per side or until cooked through. Serve as directed.

Thai Pork Satay

Prep 20 minutes **Grill** 4 minutes
Marinate 2 hours **Makes** 4 servings

1¼	pounds thick-cut boneless pork loin chops, trimmed
1	bottle (11.5-ounce) Thai peanut sauce, *House of Tsang®*
2	scallions (green onions), finely chopped
2	tablespoons finely chopped fresh cilantro
2	tablespoons chile-garlic sauce, *Lee Kum Kee®*
1	tablespoon lime juice, *ReaLime®*
2	teaspoons sesame seeds
1	teaspoon salt-free Thai seasoning, *Spice Hunter®*

1. Slice pork into ¼-inch-thick strips. Place in a large zip-top bag. In a bowl, combine peanut sauce, scallions, cilantro, the chile-garlic sauce, lime juice, sesame seeds, and Thai seasoning. Pour ⅓ cup of the peanut sauce mixture in bag. Squeeze air out of bag; seal. Gently massage bag. Marinate in refrigerator for 2 hours to overnight. Cover and chill remaining peanut sauce mixture. Soak 6-inch wooden skewers in water for at least 1 hour.

2. Set up grill for direct cooking over medium-high heat (see page 15). Oil grate when ready to start cooking. Remove pork from marinade; discard marinade. Drain skewers. Thread pork onto skewers. Place skewers on hot, oiled grill. Cook for 2 to 4 minutes per side or until cooked through; remove from grill. Sprinkle with additional finely chopped *green onion* (optional). Serve hot with reserved peanut sauce mixture.

INDOOR METHOD:
Prepare skewers and Peanut Dipping Sauce as directed. Preheat broiler. Place skewers on a wire rack over a foil-lined baking sheet or broiler pan. Broil 6 to 8 inches from heat source for 2 to 3 minutes per side or until cooked through. Serve as directed.

Hula Hula Pork Kabobs

Prep 20 minutes **Grill** 16 minutes
Marinate 2 hours **Makes** 4 servings

Here's a fun way to have a luau-style meal without roasting a pig. Grilling pineapple caramelizes the sugar on the surface to bring out its juicy flavor.

1¼	pounds pork tenderloin, trimmed
¼	cup sesame-ginger marinade, *Lawry's®*
¼	cup chili sauce, *Heinz®*
¼	cup soy sauce, *Kikkoman®*
¼	cup dry sherry, *Christian Brothers®*
½	cup fresh pineapple wedges, cut into 1-inch cubes, *Ready Pac®*
1	green bell pepper, cut into 1-inch cubes

1. Cut pork into 1-inch cubes. Place pork cubes in a large zip-top bag; set aside. For marinade, in a bowl, combine sesame-ginger marinade, chili sauce, soy sauce, and sherry. Reserve ½ cup of the marinade for basting; pour remaining into bag with pork. Squeeze air out of bag; seal. Gently massage bag to combine. Marinate in refrigerator for 2 hours to overnight.

2. Soak 10-inch wooden skewers in water for at least 1 hour. Set up grill for direct cooking over medium-high heat (see page 15). Oil grate when ready to start cooking. Remove pork from marinade; discard marinade in bag. Thread pork, pineapple, and pepper onto skewers. Place skewers on hot, oiled grill. Cook for 4 to 6 minutes per side (16 to 24 minutes total) or until pork is cooked through, basting with reserved marinade for the first 10 minutes of cooking time. Discard remaining marinade. Serve hot.

INDOOR METHOD:
Prepare as directed. Preheat broiler. Place skewers on a wire rack over a foil-lined baking sheet. Broil 6 to 8 inches from heat source for 3 to 5 minutes per side (12 to 20 minutes total) or until pork is cooked through, basting with reserved marinade for the first 8 minutes of cooking time. Discard marinade.

Lamb Kefta Skewers

Prep 25 minutes
Grill 12 minutes
Makes 4 servings

8	8- to 10-inch fresh rosemary stalks
1½	pounds ground lamb
¼	cup chopped fresh flat-leaf parsley
2	teaspoons chopped fresh rosemary
1	teaspoon garlic salt, *Lawry's*®
1	teaspoon garam masala, *Spice Hunter*® (see note, page 83)
½	teaspoon ground black pepper, *McCormick*®
24	garlic-stuffed green olives, *Santa Barbara*®
4	pita bread rounds, *Sara Lee*®
	Purchased tzatziki sauce

INDOOR METHOD:

Prepare skewers as directed. Preheat oven to 375 degrees F. Place skewers on a foil-lined baking sheet. Bake in oven for 30 to 35 minutes or until cooked through.

1. Strip all but the top 1 inch of leaves from the rosemary stalks. Wrap the tops in aluminum foil. In a bowl, thoroughly combine ground lamb, parsley, chopped rosemary, garlic salt, garam masala, and pepper. Form into 16 meatballs. Alternately thread olives and meatballs on the rosemary stalks. Set up grill for direct cooking over medium-high heat (see page 15). Oil grate when ready to start cooking. Place skewers on hot, oiled grill. Cook for 12 to 15 minutes or until cooked through, turning often. Serve hot with pita bread and tzatziki sauce.

Chicken Yakitori

Prep 20 minutes   **Grill** 8 minutes
Marinate 2 hours   **Makes** 4 servings

Yakitori is grilled chicken skewered on sticks. In Japan, it's traditionally served with tare—a sweet sake, soy, and sugar sauce. My version adds sherry, garlic, and ginger to give it a bit more bite. It begs to be paired with a frosty beer, just like they do it at yakitori stalls in Tokyo.

1	cup soy sauce, *Kikkoman*®
½	cup sake, *Sho Chiko Bai*®
¼	cup dry sherry, *Christian Brothers*®
2	tablespoons minced ginger, *Gourmet Garden*®
2	teaspoons crushed garlic, *Gourmet Garden*®
2	teaspoons toasted sesame oil
1¼	pounds boneless, skinless chicken breast halves
3	bunches scallions (green onions), cut into 1-inch-long pieces

INDOOR METHOD:

Prepare yakitori sauce and skewers as directed. Preheat broiler. Place skewers on a wire rack over a foil-lined baking sheet. Broil 6 to 8 inches from heat source for 2 to 3 minutes per side (8 to 12 minutes total) or until chicken is no longer pink and juices run clear, brushing with reserved yakitori sauce during first 6 minutes of cooking. Serve hot.

1. For yakitori sauce, in a medium bowl, combine soy sauce, sake, sherry, ginger, garlic, and sesame oil. Cut chicken into 1-inch cubes. Place in a large zip-top bag. Pour 1 cup of the yakitori sauce into bag. Reserve remaining yakitori sauce for brushing. Squeeze air out of bag; seal. Gently massage bag to combine. Marinate in refrigerator for 2 to 6 hours.

2. Soak 8-inch wooden skewers in water for at least 1 hour. Set up grill for direct cooking over medium heat (see page 15). Oil grate when ready to start cooking. Remove chicken from marinade; discard marinade. Drain skewers. Alternately thread chicken and 2 scallion pieces on skewers. Place on hot, oiled grill. Cook for 2 to 3 minutes per side (8 to 12 minutes total) or until chicken is no longer pink and juices run clear, brushing liberally with reserved yakitori sauce during the first 6 minutes of grilling. Discard remaining yakitori sauce. Serve hot.

Lemongrass Chicken Skewers

Prep 25 minutes
Grill 12 minutes
Makes 4 servings

Instead of being basted with a glaze, ground chicken is mixed with ginger, garlic and clean, citrusy lemongrass to give it a spring-fresh taste. A punch of pimiento keeps the sweetness in check. Grill these on wispy lemongrass stalks to make a pretty plate for a luncheon or brunch.

1	pound ground chicken
1	jar (2-ounce) diced pimiento, drained, *Dromedary®*
1	tablespoon finely chopped fresh cilantro
1	tablespoon lemongrass blend, *Gourmet Garden®*
2	teaspoons minced ginger, *Gourmet Garden®*
1	teaspoon salt
1	teaspoon curry powder, *McCormick®*
1	teaspoon crushed garlic, *Gourmet Garden®*
8	lemongrass stalks, rinsed

FOR LEMONGRASS CURRY DIPPING SAUCE:

½	cup sour cream, *Knudsen®*
1	tablespoon lemongrass blend, *Gourmet Garden®*
1	teaspoon curry powder, *McCormick®*
1	teaspoon minced ginger, *Gourmet Garden®*
½	teaspoon lime juice, *ReaLime®*
¼	teaspoon salt

1. In a large bowl, combine ground chicken, drained pimiento, cilantro, 1 tablespoon lemongrass blend, the 2 teaspoons ginger, the 1 teaspoon salt, 1 teaspoon curry powder, and the crushed garlic. Mix thoroughly. Divide chicken mixture into 8 equal portions; tightly form each portion into an egg shape over the bulb end of a lemongrass stalk. Set aside.

2. For Lemongrass Curry Dipping Sauce, in a small bowl, combine sour cream, 1 tablespoon lemongrass blend, 1 teaspoon curry powder, the 1 teaspoon ginger, the lime juice, and the ¼ teaspoon salt. Cover and chill until ready to serve.

3. Set up grill for direct cooking over medium heat (see page 15). Oil grate when ready to start cooking. Place skewers on hot, oiled grill. Cook for 12 to 16 minutes or until cooked through, turning frequently. Serve with Lemongrass Curry Dipping Sauce.

INDOOR METHOD:
Prepare skewers and Lemongrass Curry Dipping Sauce as directed. Preheat oven to 375 degrees F. Place skewers on a foil-lined baking sheet. Bake in oven for 30 to 35 minutes or until cooked through. Serve as directed.

Tuscan Turkey Meatball Kabobs

Prep 20 minutes
Grill 12 minutes
Makes 4 servings

These easy-to-eat kabobs reinvent meat loaf for the grill, giving it a Tuscan twist that's health-conscious enough to please adults and sweet enough to delight the younger crowd. They're perfect for parties—you can assemble them in advance and grill them up in about 10 minutes.

FOR TURKEY MEATBALLS:
1¼   pounds ground turkey
1   jar (2-ounce) diced pimiento, drained, *Dromedary*®
¼   cup balsamic vinaigrette, *Newman's Own*®
1   packet (1.3-ounce) Parma rosa sauce mix, *Knorr*®
5   teaspoons Italian seasoning, *McCormick*®
1½   teaspoons crushed garlic, *Gourmet Garden*®

FOR KABOBS:
1   red bell pepper, cut into 1-inch squares
1   green bell pepper, cut into 1-inch squares
½   of a red onion, cut into 1-inch squares

FOR MARINARA DIPPING SAUCE:
1   cup marinara sauce, *Barilla*®

1. Soak four 12-inch wooden skewers in water for at least 1 hour. For Turkey Meatballs, in a large bowl, combine turkey, drained pimiento, 2 tablespoons of the balsamic vinaigrette, the sauce mix, 1 tablespoon of the Italian seasoning, and 1 teaspoon of the garlic. Mix thoroughly. Form into 16 meatballs. Drain skewers. Alternately thread Turkey Meatballs, bell pepper squares, and red onion onto skewers.

2. Set up grill for direct cooking over medium heat (see page 15). Oil grate when ready to start cooking. Place skewers on hot, oiled grill. Cook for 12 to 15 minutes or until cooked through, turning frequently.

3. Meanwhile, for Marinara Dipping Sauce, in a small saucepan, stir together marinara sauce, the remaining 2 tablespoons balsamic vinaigrette, the remaining 2 teaspoons Italian seasoning, and the remaining ½ teaspoon garlic. Simmer over medium heat for 10 minutes. Serve skewers hot with Marinara Dipping Sauce.

INDOOR METHOD:
Prepare skewers and Marinara Dipping Sauce as directed. Preheat oven to 375 degrees F. Place skewers on a foil-lined baking sheet. Bake for 30 to 35 minutes or until cooked through. Serve as directed.

Bacon-Wrapped Shrimp Skewers

Prep 25 minutes
Grill 8 minutes
Makes 4 servings

12   cherry tomatoes
12   jumbo shrimp, peeled with tails left on, cleaned
4   slices bacon, cut into 3-inch pieces, *Oscar Mayer®*
2   tablespoons barbecue sauce, *Jack Daniel's®*
½   cup sour cream, *Knudsen®*
¼   cup barbecue sauce, *Jack Daniel's®*
1   tablespoon ranch salad dressing mix, *Hidden Valley®*

1. Soak twelve 6-inch wooden skewers and 12 wooden toothpicks in water for at least 1 hour. Drain skewers and toothpicks. Thread each skewer with a cherry tomato and one shrimp, threading shrimp from the head end through to the tail so that the shrimp straightens out. Brush one side of each bacon piece with some of the 2 tablespoons barbecue sauce; wrap a bacon piece, sauce side in, around each shrimp, securing with a soaked toothpick. Set up grill for direct cooking over medium heat (see page 15). Oil grate when ready to start cooking. For the dipping sauce, in a bowl, stir together sour cream, the ¼ cup barbecue sauce, and the salad dressing mix. Cover and chill until ready to serve. Place skewers on hot, oiled grill. Cook shrimp for 4 to 5 minutes per side or until shrimp are opaque and cooked through and bacon is crispy. Remove from grill. Serve hot with dipping sauce.

INDOOR METHOD:

Prepare skewers and Sour Cream Dipping Sauce as directed. Preheat broiler. Place skewers on a wire rack over a foil-lined baking sheet or broiler pan. Broil 6 to 8 inches from heat source for 3 to 4 minutes per side or until shrimp are opaque and cooked through and bacon is crispy. Serve as directed.

Tropical Shrimp Kabobs

Prep 20 minutes   Grill 12 minutes
Marinate 30 minutes   Makes 4 servings

FOR MARINADE:
1   can (11.5-ounce) mango nectar, *Kerns®*
½   cup passion fruit rum, *Malibu®*
2   tablespoons finely chopped fresh cilantro
1   packet (1-ounce) chicken taco seasoning mix, *McCormick®*

FOR SKEWERS:
24   large shrimp, peeled with tails left on
1   cup hoisin sauce, *Lee Kum Kee®*
2   red bell peppers, cut into 1-inch squares
24   frozen mango chunks, thawed, *Dole®*
24   fresh pineapple chunks, *Ready Pac®*

1. For marinade, in a small bowl, combine 1 cup of the mango nectar, the rum, cilantro, and taco seasoning mix. Place shrimp in large zip-top bag. Pour marinade over shrimp in bag. Squeeze air out of bag; seal. Massage bag to coat shrimp. Marinate in refrigerator for 30 minutes to 2 hours.

2. Soak eight 12-inch wooden skewers in water for at least 1 hour; drain. For basting sauce, in a small bowl, combine the remaining mango nectar and the hoisin sauce; set aside. Set up grill for direct cooking over medium heat (see page 15). Oil grate when ready to start cooking. Remove shrimp from marinade; discard marinade. Alternately thread shrimp, bell pepper squares, mango, and pineapple onto skewers. Place skewers on hot, oiled grill. Cook for 3 to 4 minutes per side (12 to 16 minutes total) or until shrimp are opaque and cooked through. Brush skewers with basting sauce during the last 5 minutes of cooking. Serve hot.

INDOOR METHOD:

Prepare skewers and basting sauce as directed. Preheat broiler. Place skewers on a wire rack over a foil-lined baking sheet or broiler pan. Broil 6 to 8 inches from heat source for 2 to 3 minutes per side (8 to 12 minutes total) or until shrimp are opaque and cooked through. Brush with basting sauce during last 2 minutes of cooking.

Seafood Brochettes with Cucumber Raita

Prep 30 minutes
Grill 8 minutes
Makes 4 servings

FOR SEAFOOD SPRINKLE:

1   tablespoon garlic salt, *Lawry's®*
2   teaspoons seasoned-pepper blend, *McCormick®*
2   teaspoons salt-free citrus-herb seasoning, *Spice Islands®*

FOR CUCUMBER RAITA:

⅓   cup sour cream, *Knudsen®*
⅓   cup plain yogurt, *Dannon®*
¼   cup finely diced red bell pepper
¼   cup finely diced cucumber
2   teaspoons finely chopped fresh tarragon
1   teaspoon lemon juice, *Minute Maid®*

FOR SEAFOOD BROCHETTES:

1   8-ounce center cut salmon fillet
1   8-ounce halibut fillet
8   sea scallops
½   of a red onion, cut into 1-inch squares
1   red bell pepper, cut into 1-inch squares
1   green bell pepper, cut into 1-inch squares
8   cherry tomatoes
1   tablespoon lemon juice, *Minute Maid®*
     Nonstick vegetable cooking spray, *Pam®*

1. Soak four 12-inch wooden skewers in water for at least 1 hour; drain. Meanwhile, for Seafood Sprinkle, in a small bowl, stir to combine garlic salt, pepper blend, and citrus-herb seasoning. Set aside.

2. For Cucumber Raita, in a medium bowl, stir together sour cream, yogurt, the ¼ cup red bell pepper, the cucumber, tarragon, and the 1 teaspoon lemon juice. Cover and chill until ready to serve.

3. Set up grill for direct cooking over medium heat (see page 15). Oil grate when ready to start cooking. For Seafood Brochettes, cut salmon and halibut into 1-inch cubes. Drain skewers. Alternately thread salmon, scallops, onion squares, bell pepper squares, and tomatoes on skewers, beginning and ending each skewer with a tomato. Sprinkle skewers with the 1 tablespoon lemon juice and the Seafood Sprinkle. Lightly spray with cooking spray.

4. Place skewers on hot, oiled grill. Cook for 2 to 3 minutes per side (8 to 12 minutes total) or until scallops are opaque and fish flakes easily when tested with a fork. Serve hot with Cucumber Raita.

INDOOR METHOD:
Prepare Seafood Sprinkle, Cucumber Raita, and Seafood Brochettes as directed. Preheat broiler. Place skewers on foil-lined baking sheet or broiler pan. Broil 6 to 8 inches from heat source for 2 to 3 minutes per side (8 to 12 minutes total) or until scallops are opaque and fish flakes easily when tested with a fork. Serve as directed.

Dogs and Sausages

Ballpark franks. Deli dogs. Wisconsin bratwurst. This chapter has them all, from a Varsity drive-in dawg with Southern slaw to fashion's haute dog—a French frank with Brie on a baguette. Plus everything in between such as a spicy Mexican-style dog complete with refried beans, salsa, and a fiery cheese, or a trendy sausage pizza piled with gourmet favorites such as fennel, roasted red peppers, and plenty of mozzarella cheese. You can even make it supersimple by teaching your plain old dogs new tricks by making over ketchup and mustard. Just add some flavorful herbs, spices, or seasoning blends to these all-time favorite hot dog condiments, slather on plain franks, add a bun or sourdough roll, and you've just designed dinner's top dog!

The Recipes

Dressing Up Condiments

Spice up the usual ho-hum ketchup by stirring in your favorite seasonings or spices. To ½ cup ketchup, add one of the following: 1 teaspoon seafood seasoning (*Old Bay®*), celery salt, or any seasoning blend (*McCormick®*); or 1 tablespoon taco seasoning mix (*McCormick®*) or garlic and herb sauce mix (*McCormick®*).

And what about the hot dog's favorite condiment, mustard? Try this: to ½ cup yellow or brown mustard add ¼ cup honey, 1 tablespoon hoisin sauce, ½ teaspoon fresh snipped dill, ¼ teaspoon prepared horseradish, or a splash of juice from jarred jalapeño chile peppers.

Ball Park Dogs

Prep 20 minutes
Grill 12 minutes
Makes 4 servings

4   hot dog buns, *Ball Park®*
1   egg, beaten
1   tablespoon poppy seeds
¼   cup sweet pickle relish, *Vlassic®*
2   drops green food coloring, *McCormick®*
4   all-beef franks, *Ball Park®*
    Yellow mustard, *French's®*
⅓   cup frozen chopped onions, thawed, *Ore Ida®*
1   tomato, cut into 8 wedges
4   pickle spears, *Vlassic®*

INDOOR METHOD:
Prepare buns and relish as directed. Preheat broiler. Place franks on a wire rack over a foil-lined baking sheet or broiler pan. Broil 6 to 8 inches from heat source for 12 to 15 minutes, turning occasionally. Serve franks as directed.

1. Preheat oven to 350 degrees F. Very lightly brush bun tops with egg and sprinkle with poppy seeds. Bake in oven for 10 minutes. Remove from oven; set aside. Meanwhile, combine relish and food coloring; set aside. Set up grill for direct cooking over medium heat (see page 15). Oil grate when ready to start cooking. Place franks on hot, oiled grill. Cook for 12 to 15 minutes or until heated through, turning occasionally. Place franks in buns; top with mustard. Top each frank with some of the relish mixture and onions. Arrange two tomato wedges between each frank and top of bun. Place a pickle spear between each frank and bottom of bun.

TIP: Order authentic Chicago bright-green sweet relish, pickle spears, and sport peppers online from The Puckered Pickle at www.puckeredpickle.com.

Varsity Dogs

Prep 15 minutes
Grill 12 minutes
Makes 4 servings

FOR SOUTHERN SLAW:
3   tablespoons cider vinegar, *Heinz®*
2   teaspoons ranch salad dressing mix, *Hidden Valley®*
2   teaspoons sugar
2   cups tricolor coleslaw mix, *Fresh Express®*

FOR VARSITY DOGS:
4   all-beef franks, *Ball Park®*
4   hot dogs buns, *Ball Park®*
4   slices American cheese, *Borden®*
1   cup chili without beans, heated, *Hormel®*

INDOOR METHOD:
Prepare Southern Slaw as directed. Preheat broiler. Place franks on a wire rack over a foil-lined baking sheet. Cook 6 to 8 inches from heat source for 12 to 15 minutes or until heated through, turning occasionally. Serve as directed.

1. For Southern Slaw, in a medium bowl, stir together vinegar, salad dressing mix, and sugar. Add coleslaw mix and toss. Cover; chill until ready to use.

2. For Varsity Dogs, set up grill for direct cooking over medium heat (see page 15). Oil grate when ready to start cooking. Grill franks on hot, oiled grill for 12 to 15 minutes or until heated through, turning occasionally. Remove and set aside. Toast buns on grill until golden brown. Remove and add cheese slices to hot buns. Spoon Southern Slaw in buns; place franks on slaw and top with warm chili.

Sonora Dogs

Prep 15 minutes
Grill 16 minutes
Makes 4 servings

4	hearty beef franks, *Ball Park®*
4	slices bacon, *Oscar Mayer®*
½	of an onion, thickly sliced
4	sourdough rolls, split horizontally and toasted, *Francisco®*
½	cup refried beans, heated, *Rosarita®*
½	cup bottled chunky salsa, *Ortega®*
½	cup sour cream, *Knudsen®*
½	cup prepared guacamole, *Calavo®*
	Nacho rings, *Ortega®* (optional)

1. Set up grill for direct cooking over medium heat (see page 15). Oil grate when ready to start cooking. Wrap each frank in a slice of bacon, securing the ends with wooden toothpicks.

2. Place bacon-wrapped franks and onion slices on hot, oiled grill. Cook for 16 to 20 minutes or until bacon is crispy, turning often. Turn onion slices each time you turn the franks. Serve franks and onion hot on toasted rolls. Top with beans, salsa, sour cream, and guacamole. Add nacho rings (optional).

INDOOR METHOD:
Prepare franks and onion slices as directed. Preheat broiler. Place franks and onion slices on wire rack over foil-lined baking sheet or broiler pan. Broil 4 to 6 inches from heat source for 16 to 20 minutes or until bacon is crispy, turning frequently. Turn onion slices each time you turn the franks. Serve as directed.

Reuben Dogs

Prep 15 minutes
Grill 12 minutes
Makes 4 servings

4	all-beef big franks, *Hebrew National®*
4	teaspoons spicy brown mustard, *Gulden's®*
12	slices deli pastrami, *Hillshire Farm®*
4	sourdough French rolls, halved horizontally and toasted, *Francisco®*
4	slices Swiss cheese, cut in half diagonally
1	cup prepared sauerkraut, *Boar's Head®*
	Thousand Island salad dressing, *Wish-Bone®*

1. Set up grill for direct cooking over medium heat (see page 15). Oil grate when ready to start cooking. Spread each frank on all sides with 1 teaspoon mustard. Wrap three slices of the pastrami around each frank.

2. Grill pastrami-wrapped franks on hot, oiled grill. Cook for 12 to 16 minutes or until heated through, turning frequently. Serve franks hot on toasted French rolls with sliced cheese and sauerkraut. Top with Thousand Island salad dressing.

INDOOR METHOD:
Prepare franks as directed. Preheat broiler. Place franks on a wire rack over a foil-lined baking sheet or broiler pan. Cook 6 to 8 inches from heat source for 12 to 16 minutes, turning frequently. Serve as directed.

Saucy White Hots

Prep 15 minutes Cook 45 minutes
Grill 12 minutes Makes 4 servings

FOR MEAT SAUCE:
8 ounces lean ground beef
1 can (14-ounce) lower-sodium beef broth, *Swanson®*
½ cup chili sauce, *Heinz®*
2 tablespoons frozen chopped onions, thawed, *Ore Ida®*
1 teaspoon spicy Montreal steak seasoning, *McCormick® Grill Mates®*
¼ teaspoon ground cinnamon, *McCormick®*

FOR WHITE HOTS:
4 bratwursts, *Johnsonville® Stadium-Style*
4 French rolls, toasted, *Francisco®*

INDOOR METHOD:
Prepare Meat Sauce as directed. Preheat broiler. Place bratwursts on a wire rack over a foil-lined baking sheet or broiler pan. Broil 6 to 8 inches from heat source for 10 to 12 minutes or until done (160 degrees F), turning occasionally. Serve as directed.

1. In a large skillet, combine ground beef, beef broth, chili sauce, the 2 tablespoons onion, steak seasoning, and cinnamon. Cook over medium heat, stirring to break up meat into fine pieces. Reduce heat; simmer gently for 45 minutes to 1 hour or until liquid is evaporated. Set up grill for direct cooking over medium heat (see page 15). Oil grate when ready to start cooking. Place bratwursts on hot, oiled grill. Cook for 12 to 15 minutes or until done (160 degrees F), turning occasionally. Serve hot on toasted rolls. Top with the meat sauce and additional chopped onion.

French Dogs

Prep 15 minutes
Grill 16 minutes
Makes 4 servings

FOR MUSHROOM KETCHUP:
1 tablespoon extra-virgin olive oil, *Bertolli®*
¼ cup finely chopped cremini mushrooms
1 teaspoon fines herbes, *Spice Islands®*
½ teaspoon crushed garlic, *Gourmet Garden®*
½ cup ketchup, *Heinz®*
1 tablespoon dry sherry, *Christian Brothers®*

FOR FRENCH DOGS:
1 sweet onion, thickly sliced
1 tablespoon extra-virgin olive oil, *Bertolli®*
4 portobello sausages, *Aidells®*
4 mini baguettes or French rolls, split horizontally and toasted
4 ounces Brie cheese, sliced

INDOOR METHOD:
Prepare Mushroom Ketchup as directed. In a large skillet, heat 2 tablespoons olive oil over medium heat. Add onion slices and sausages. Cook for 15 to 18 minutes or until sausages are done (160 degrees F) and onion slices are softened, turning often. Serve as directed.

1. In a small skillet, heat 1 tablespoon oil over medium-high heat. Add mushrooms, fines herbes, and garlic. Cook until mushrooms are softened and have released their juices. Transfer to a blender; add ketchup and sherry. Cover; puree until smooth. Set up grill for direct cooking over medium heat (see page 15). Oil grate when ready to start cooking. In a bowl, toss onion slices with 1 tablespoon oil. Place sausages and onion slices on hot, oiled grill. Cook for 16 to 20 minutes or until sausages are done (160 degrees F) and onion slices are softened, turning often. Serve sausages on baguettes with Brie, onion, and Mushroom Ketchup.

Perro Caliente

Prep 15 minutes
Grill 12 minutes
Makes 4 servings

Perro Caliente is, literally, "hot dog" in Spanish, and a spirited combo of green chile sausages, chipotle cheddar cheese, and spicy salsa make it hot indeed!

4	habañero-and-green chile sausages, *Aidells®*
4	taco-size flour tortillas, *Mission®*
4	slices chipotle cheddar cheese, *Sargento®*
1	cup precooked Spanish rice, heated, *Uncle Ben's® Ready Rice®*
1	cup refried black beans, heated, *Rosarita®*
⅓	cup bottled chunky salsa, *Ortega®*

1. Set up grill for direct cooking over medium heat (see page 15). Oil grate when ready to cook. Place sausages on hot, oiled grill. Cook for 12 to 15 minutes or until done (160 degrees F), turning occasionally; remove.

2. Toast tortillas on grill for about 10 seconds per side, using tongs to turn tortillas. Remove and place a slice of cheese in the center of each tortilla. Add a sausage to each tortilla. Top each with some of the Spanish rice, black beans, and salsa. For each, with the sausage parallel to the edge of the counter, fold over sides. Fold bottom edge over sausage and roll over.

INDOOR METHOD:
Preheat broiler. Place sausages on a wire rack over a foil-lined baking sheet or broiler pan. Broil 6 to 8 inches from heat source for 12 to 15 minutes or until done (160 degrees F), turning occasionally. Toast tortillas on stovetop, allowing 10 seconds per side, using tongs to carefully turn tortillas. Serve as directed.

Chicken Sausages with Raspberry Mustard

Prep 15 minutes
Grill 16 minutes
Makes 4 servings

FOR RASPBERRY MUSTARD:

1	cup frozen raspberries, thawed, *Dole®*
½	cup spicy brown mustard, *Gulden's®*
3	tablespoons raspberry preserves, *Smucker's®*
1	teaspoon raspberry vinegar, *Kozlowski Farms®*

FOR CHICKEN SAUSAGE SANDWICHES:

1	fennel bulb, cut into ¼-inch-thick slices
1	sweet onion, cut into ¼-inch-thick slices
1	tablespoon extra-virgin olive oil, *Bertolli®*
4	chicken-and-apple sausages, *Aidells®*
4	French sandwich rolls, toasted, *Francisco®*

1. In a blender, combine raspberries, mustard, preserves, and vinegar. Cover; puree until smooth. Set aside. For Chicken Sausage Sandwiches, set up grill for direct cooking over medium heat (see page 15). Oil grate when ready to start cooking. In a large bowl, toss fennel and onion slices with olive oil and a little *salt* and *ground black pepper*.

2. Place sausages, fennel, and onion slices on hot, oiled grill. Cook for 16 to 20 minutes or until vegetables are softened and sausages are done (160 degrees F). Turn vegetables every time you turn sausages. Serve sausages hot on toasted French rolls piled with fennel and onions. Top with Raspberry Mustard.

INDOOR METHOD:
Prepare Raspberry Mustard and vegetables as directed. Heat a large skillet over medium heat. Add vegetables and sausages. Cook for 12 to 15 minutes or until vegetables have softened and sausages are heated through.

Sausage, Fennel, and Red Pepper Pizza

Prep 15 minutes
Grill 10 minutes
Makes 4 servings

1	can (13.8-ounce) refrigerated pizza crust dough, *Pillsbury®*
½	cup Cabernet marinara sauce, *Newman's Own®*
8	ounces fresh mozzarella cheese packed in water, cut into ¼-inch-thick slices, *Cantaré®*
1	medium fennel bulb, thinly sliced
½	cup roasted red bell peppers, cut into strips, *Delallo®*
2	fully cooked artichoke-and-garlic sausages, cut into ¼-inch-thick diagonal slices, *Aidells®*
¼	cup shredded Parmesan cheese, *DiGiorno®*

INDOOR METHOD:

Preheat oven to 425 degrees F. Lightly spray cookie sheet with nonstick vegetable cooking spray (*Pam®*). Carefully unroll dough and place on prepared cookie sheet. Press out pizza dough with fingers to form 13×9-inch rectangle. Bake in oven about 7 minutes or just until crust begins to brown. Remove crust from oven and top as directed in step 3. Return to oven for 8 to 10 minutes or until crust is golden brown and cheese is bubbly and melted.

1. Set up grill for direct cooking over medium heat (see page 15). Oil grate when ready to start cooking.

2. Carefully remove pizza dough from can. Unroll pizza dough and place on hot, oiled grill. Cook for 2 minutes. Using a cookie sheet as a spatula, turn crust over.

3. Spread marinara sauce over crust, leaving a 1-inch border. Top with mozzarella cheese, fennel, bell pepper, sausage pieces, and Parmesan cheese. Cover grill. Cook for 8 to 10 minutes or until cheese is bubbly and melted. Using cookie sheet, remove from grill. Serve hot.

Grilled Sausage-and-Summer Vegetable Pasta

Prep 25 minutes
Grill 18 minutes
Makes 6 servings

1	package (16-ounce) penne pasta, *Barilla®*
8	ounces fresh asparagus, trimmed
1	red bell pepper, cut into strips
1	zucchini, cut in half lengthwise and sliced
1	yellow squash, cut in half lengthwise and sliced
½	of a red onion, thickly sliced
1	tablespoon extra-virgin olive oil, *Bertolli®*
	Salt
	Ground black pepper, *McCormick®*
4	hot Italian sausages
¼	cup extra-virgin olive oil, *Bertolli®*
1	tablespoon Italian salad dressing mix, *Good Seasons®*
1	teaspoon crushed garlic, *Gourmet Garden®*
	Shredded Parmesan cheese, *DiGiorno®*

1. Cook pasta according to package directions; drain. Set aside. Set up grill for direct cooking over medium heat (see page 15). Oil grate when ready to start cooking. In a large bowl, toss asparagus, bell pepper, zucchini, yellow squash, and onion with the 1 tablespoon oil. Season to taste with salt and black pepper.

2. Place sausages and vegetables on hot, oiled grill (use a vegetable grilling basket if desired). Watch for flare-ups when putting vegetables on grill. Cook for 18 to 20 minutes or until sausages are done (160 degrees F) and vegetables are al dente, turning sausages and vegetables often.

3. Remove sausages and vegetables from grill. Carefully slice sausages diagonally. In a large bowl, combine cooked pasta, sliced sausages, and vegetables.

4. In a small bowl, stir together the ¼ cup oil, the salad dressing mix, and garlic. Pour over pasta and toss. Serve hot topped with Parmesan cheese.

INDOOR METHOD:
Preheat oven to 400 degrees F. Prepare vegetables as directed. Place vegetables and sausages in a foil-lined baking pan. Roast in oven for 10 to 15 minutes or until sausages are done (160 degrees F) and vegetables are al dente. Serve as directed.

Pork and Lamb

Whether it's whiskey-laced spareribs or a jerked pork sandwich, slow-roasted, well-seasoned pork has become the house dish of the South. This chapter broadens the focus, with 12 popular pork and lamb entrees that deliver a world of slow-cooked flavor fast.

Made in five minutes with pantry spices, my All-Purpose Pork Rub adds a lot of flavor for little effort … or combine it with liquid marinades and sauces for an explosion of flavors. Brush my Backwoods BBQ Sauce on rubbed spareribs or baby backs to blacken the spices into a crispy crust. Beer-brine pork chops, then rub right before grilling to deepen flavors with a one-two punch. Drizzle sherry-soaked lamb with a ginger glaze … or spatchcook it with yogurt and tandoori spices. Blazin' hot or sweet as sugar—you choose, then rub, sauce, sizzle, and serve!

The Recipes

All-Purpose Pork Rub

Prep 5 minutes **Makes** ¾ cup

- 2   packets (0.7 ounce each) Italian salad dressing mix, *Good Seasons*®
- ¼   cup paprika, *McCormick*®
- ¼   cup chili powder, *Gebhardt's*®
- 2   tablespoons packed brown sugar, *C&H*®
- 2   tablespoons salt-free lemon pepper, *McCormick*®

1. In a small bowl, combine salad dressing mix, paprika, chili powder, brown sugar, and lemon pepper. Transfer to an airtight container. Store at room temperature for up to 3 months.

Pork Loin with Honey-Mustard Glaze

Prep 15 minutes   **Grill** 1 hour
Stand 40 minutes   **Marinate** 6 hours
Makes 6 servings

1	3-pound pork loin
¼	cup extra-virgin olive oil, *Bertolli*®
3	tablespoons Dijon mustard, *Grey Poupon*®
2	tablespoons honey, *SueBee*®
1	packet (0.4-ounce) ranch-style dressing mix, *Hidden Valley*®
1	tablespoon red wine vinegar, *Pompeian*®

FOR HONEY-MUSTARD GLAZE:

½	cup Dijon mustard, *Grey Poupon*®
¼	cup honey, *SueBee*®
2	tablespoons lemon juice, *Minute Maid*®
1	tablespoon soy sauce, *Kikkoman*®

1. Place pork loin in large zip-top bag. For marinade, in a small bowl, combine oil, the 3 tablespoons mustard, the 2 tablespoons honey, salad dressing mix, and vinegar. Pour over pork in bag. Squeeze air out of bag; seal. Gently massage bag to coat pork. Marinate in refrigerator for 6 to 12 hours.

2. Set up grill for indirect cooking over medium heat (no heat source under pork; see page 15). Oil grate when ready to start cooking. Remove pork from marinade; discard marinade. Let pork stand at room temperature for 30 minutes.

3. For Honey-Mustard Glaze, in a medium bowl, whisk together the ½ cup mustard, the ¼ cup honey, the lemon juice, and soy sauce. Set aside.

4. Place pork on hot, oiled grill over drip pan. Cover grill. Cook for 1 to 1½ hours or until slightly pink in center and juices run clear (150 degrees F). If using charcoal, add 10 briquettes to each pile of coals after 1 hour. Brush roast with Honey-Mustard Glaze every 10 minutes after the first hour of cooking.

5. Remove from grill. Brush with Honey-Mustard Glaze. Let stand for 10 minutes before slicing. Serve hot.

INDOOR METHOD:
Prepare pork as directed. Preheat oven to 450 degrees F. Remove pork from marinade; discard marinade. Place pork on a wire rack in a roasting pan. Place in oven and immediately reduce heat to 325 degrees F. Roast for 1¼ to 1½ hours (about 25 minutes per pound) or until slightly pink in center and juices run clear (150 degrees F). Brush with Honey-Mustard Glaze every 10 minutes during the final 30 minutes of roasting. Remove from oven and tent with aluminum foil. Let stand for 10 minutes before slicing.

Pork Chops with Corn and Red Pepper Relish

Prep 20 minutes
Grill 12 minutes
Makes 4 servings

2	tablespoons paprika, *McCormick®*
2	tablespoons salt-free chicken seasoning, *McCormick® Grill Mates®*
1	tablespoon chili powder, *Gebhardt's®*
1	tablespoon Montreal steak seasoning, *McCormick® Grill Mates®*
4	center-cut bone-in pork chops, ½ inch thick

FOR CORN AND RED PEPPER RELISH:

1	can (11-ounce) no-salt-added corn kernels, drained, *Green Giant®*
½	cup roasted red bell pepper, chopped, *Delallo®*
1	tablespoon diced canned jalapeño chile peppers, *Ortega®*
2	scallions (green onions), chopped
2	tablespoons red wine vinegar, *Pompeian®*
1	teaspoon Montreal steak seasoning, *McCormick® Grill Mates®*
1	teaspoon sugar

1. Set up grill for direct cooking over medium-high heat (see page 15). Oil grate when ready to start cooking.

2. In a small bowl, stir together paprika, chicken seasoning, chili powder, and 1 tablespoon steak seasoning. Rub into pork chops; set aside.

3. For Corn and Red Pepper Relish, in a medium bowl, combine drained corn, red pepper, jalapeño chile pepper, scallions, vinegar, the 1 teaspoon steak seasoning, and sugar. Set aside.

4. Place chops on hot, oiled grill. Cook for 6 to 7 minutes per side or until slightly pink in centers and juices run clear (160 degrees F). Serve hot with Corn and Red Pepper Relish.

INDOOR METHOD:

Prepare chops and Corn and Red Pepper Relish as directed. Preheat broiler. Place chops on foil-lined baking sheet or broiler pan. Broil 6 to 8 inches from heat source for 3 to 4 minutes per side or until slightly pink in centers and juices run clear (160 degrees F). Serve as directed.

Beer-Brined Pork Chops

Prep 10 minutes   Grill 10 minutes
Stand 30 minutes   Marinate 2 hours
Makes 4 servings

4   center-cut bone-in pork chops, 1 inch thick

FOR BEER BRINE:
2   tablespoons sugar
1   teaspoon cracked black peppercorns, *McCormick®*
1   bottle (12-ounce) lager-style beer
2   tablespoons spicy brown mustard, *Gulden's®*
2   teaspoons crushed garlic, *Gourmet Garden®*
¼   teaspoon liquid smoke, *Wright's®*

1. Place pork chops in large zip-top bag; set aside. For Beer Brine, in a small saucepan, combine ½ cup *water,* 2 tablespoons *salt,* the sugar, and peppercorns. Bring to a boil; reduce heat. Simmer until sugar and salt are dissolved. Remove from heat. Stir in beer, mustard, garlic, and liquid smoke. Pour over chops in bag. Squeeze air out of bag; seal. Gently massage bag to coat. Marinate in refrigerator for 2 to 4 hours.

2. Set up grill for direct cooking over medium heat (see page 15). Oil grate when ready to cook. Let chops stand at room temperature for 30 minutes. Remove chops from brine and pat dry with paper towels. Discard brine. Lightly spray both sides of the chops with *nonstick vegetable cooking spray.* Place chops on hot, oiled grill. Cook for 5 to 6 minutes per side or until slightly pink in centers and juices run clear (160 degrees F). Serve hot.

INDOOR METHOD:
Prepare chops as directed. Preheat broiler. Place chops on foil-lined baking sheet or broiler pan. Broil 6 to 8 inches from heat source for 5 to 6 minutes per side or until slightly pink in center and juices run clear (160 degrees F). Serve as directed.

Salami-Stuffed Pork Chops

Prep 20 minutes
Grill 10 minutes
Makes 4 servings

4   boneless pork loin chops, cut 1 inch thick, trimmed

FOR SALAMI-AND-OLIVE STUFFING:
⅓   cup olive tapenade, *Cantaré®*
⅓   cup chopped salami, *Gallo®*
2   tablespoons grated Parmesan cheese, *DiGiorno®*
1   tablespoon chopped fresh parsley
3   teaspoons Italian seasoning, *McCormick®*
2   teaspoons Montreal steak seasoning, *McCormick® Grill Mates®*
2   teaspoons Dijon mustard, *Grey Poupon®*
1   teaspoon crushed garlic, *Gourmet Garden®*

1. Set up grill for direct cooking over medium heat (see page 15). Oil grate when ready to start cooking. Cut a pocket into the side of each pork chop. For Salami-and-Olive Stuffing, combine tapenade, salami, Parmesan cheese, parsley, 1 teaspoon of the Italian seasoning, 1 teaspoon of the steak seasoning, the mustard, and garlic. Spoon stuffing into pocket in each chop; secure pocket with wooden toothpicks. Season all sides of chops with the remaining 2 teaspoons Italian seasoning and the remaining 1 teaspoon steak seasoning.

2. Place chops on hot, oiled grill. Cook for 5 to 6 minutes per side or until slightly pink in center and juices run clear (160 degrees F). Serve hot.

INDOOR METHOD:
Prepare chops as directed. Preheat oven to 350 degrees F. Place chops on a foil-lined baking sheet. Bake in oven about 1 hour or until slightly pink in centers and juices run clear (160 degrees F). Serve hot.

Planked Pork Tenderloin

Prep 15 minutes   Grill 18 minutes
Stand 5 minutes   Makes 4 servings

FOR APPLE-SAGE GLAZE:

½   cup frozen apple juice concentrate, *Tree Top®*
2   tablespoons packed brown sugar, *C&H®*
1   tablespoon cider vinegar, *Heinz®*
1   teaspoon crushed garlic, *Gourmet Garden®*
½   teaspoon dried whole sage leaves
¼   teaspoon pumpkin pie spice, *McCormick®*
    Pinch red pepper flakes, *McCormick®*

FOR PORK:

1½   pounds pork tenderloin, trimmed
2   teaspoons Montreal steak seasoning, *McCormick® Grill Mates®*

INDOOR METHOD:
Preheat oven to 375 degrees F. Prepare Apple-Sage Glaze and pork as directed. For a smoky flavor, add 1 to 2 drops liquid smoke (*Wright's®*) to glaze. Roast in oven for 20 to 25 minutes or until slightly pink in center and juices run clear (155 degrees F), brushing with glaze every 5 minutes. Return remaining glaze to boiling. Serve as directed.

1. Soak a hickory grilling plank in water for 1 hour. Set up grill for direct cooking over medium-high heat (see page 15). In a saucepan, combine Apple-Sage Glaze ingredients. Bring to a boil over medium-high heat. Reduce to simmer, stirring constantly until sugar dissolves; set aside. Season pork with steak seasoning. Place soaked plank on hot grill; cover grill for 3 minutes, turning plank every minute. Place pork on plank; brush with glaze. Cover grill. Cook for 10 minutes, brushing with glaze every 5 minutes. Cook for 8 to 10 minutes more or until slightly pink in center and juices run clear (155 degrees F). Remove pork from grill; let stand for 5 minutes. Meanwhile, return remaining glaze to boiling. Slice pork. Serve hot drizzled with hot Apple-Sage Glaze. Top with *fresh sage* (optional).

Jerked Pork Sandwiches

Prep 20 minutes   Grill 4 minutes
Stand 20 minutes   Marinate 1 hour
Makes 4 servings

1½   pounds pork tenderloin, trimmed
1   cup pineapple juice, *Dole®*
⅓   cup dark rum, *Myers's®*
2   tablespoons Caribbean jerk seasoning, *McCormick®*

FOR CARIBBEAN MAYO:

½   cup mayonnaise, *Hellmann's®* or *Best Foods®*
1   teaspoon lemon juice, *Minute Maid®*
½   teaspoon Caribbean jerk seasoning, *McCormick®*
4   sweet Hawaiian dinner rolls, sliced, *Oroweat®*
    Lettuce leaves and grilled pineapple and onion slices (optional)

INDOOR METHOD:
Prepare pork as directed. Preheat broiler. Place pork slices on foil-lined baking sheet or broiler pan. Broil 6 to 8 inches from heat source for 3 to 5 minutes per side or until cooked through. Serve as directed.

1. Cut pork into 1-inch-thick slices; pound each to a ¼-inch thickness. Place pork in a zip-top bag. Combine pineapple juice, rum, and the 2 tablespoons jerk seasoning. Pour over pork in bag. Squeeze air out of bag; seal. Gently massage bag. Marinate in refrigerator for 1 hour. Meanwhile, combine mayonnaise, lemon juice, and the ½ teaspoon jerk seasoning. Cover; chill. Set up grill for direct cooking over medium heat (see page 15). Oil grate when ready to start cooking. Let pork stand at room temperature for 20 minutes. Remove pork from marinade; discard marinade. Place pork on hot, oiled grill. Cook for 2 to 3 minutes per side or until cooked through. Serve hot on rolls with Caribbean Mayo. Top with lettuce, pineapple, and onion (optional).

Baby Back Ribs with Old No. 7 BBQ Sauce

Prep 15 minutes
Grill 2 hours
Makes 4 servings

3	racks pork baby back ribs
⅓	cup All-Purpose Pork Rub (see page 65)
2	teaspoons dry mustard, *Coleman's*®

FOR OLD NO. 7 BBQ SAUCE:

1	bottle chili sauce, *Heinz*®
⅓	cup packed brown sugar, *C&H*®
⅓	cup whiskey, *Jack Daniel's*®
¼	cup molasses, *Grandma's*®
2	tablespoons Worcestershire sauce, *Lea & Perrins*®
2	teaspoons Montreal steak seasoning, *McCormick*® *Grill Mates*®
2	tablespoons soy sauce, *Kikkoman*®
¼	teaspoon liquid smoke, *Wright's*®

1. Soak 2 cups hickory wood chips in water for at least 1 hour. Set up grill for indirect cooking over medium heat (no heat source under ribs; see page 15).

2. Remove thin membrane from the back of ribs; set aside. In a small bowl, combine All-Purpose Pork Rub with dry mustard. Sprinkle over ribs and pat in.

3. Drain wood chips. Add some of the soaked wood chips to the smoke box if using gas grill or place chips on hot coals if using charcoal. Place ribs on rib rack on hot grill over drip pan (or place ribs, bone sides down, directly on hot grill over drip pan). Cover grill. Cook for 2 to 2½ hours. Rotate ribs around rack every 30 minutes. If using charcoal, add 10 briquettes and a handful of soaked wood chips to each pile of coals every hour. If using a gas grill, add a handful of soaked wood chips to the smoke box every hour.

4. For Old No. 7 BBQ Sauce, in a medium saucepan, combine chili sauce, brown sugar, whiskey, molasses, Worcestershire sauce, steak seasoning, soy sauce, and liquid smoke. Bring to a boil; reduce heat. Simmer for 10 minutes. Remove from heat; set aside.

5. About 20 minutes before ribs are done, remove ribs from rib rack and place, meat sides down, on grill. Generously brush with Old No. 7 BBQ Sauce; stack ribs over the drip pan. Cover and cook for 10 minutes. Turn ribs; brush with additional sauce and restack. Cook 10 minutes more or until tender. Serve hot with Old No. 7 BBQ Sauce on the side.

INDOOR METHOD:
Prepare ribs as directed. Preheat oven to 350 degrees F. Place ribs, bone sides down, on a wire rack in a shallow roasting pan. Cover tightly with aluminum foil. Bake in oven for 1 hour. Meanwhile, make Old No. 7 BBQ Sauce as directed. Remove ribs from oven and carefully drain fat from roasting pan. Continue baking ribs, uncovered, for 30 to 45 minutes more or until tender, turning and brushing occasionally with sauce during the last 20 minutes of cooking. Serve as directed.

Buffalo Baby Back Ribs

Prep 15 minutes   Grill 2 hours
Stand 30 minutes   Chill 1 hour
Makes 4 servings

Buffalo wings are the inspiration for these firecracker ribs, served with celery sticks and a side of blue cheese dressing for dipping. A tangy lemon-spice rub and a generous brush of red-hot wing sauce, simmered low and slow over fragrant hickory chips, triple layers the flavor.

3	racks pork baby back ribs
1	lemon, cut in half
2	packets (1.6 ounces each) buffalo wing seasoning mix, *McCormick®*
2	teaspoons garlic powder
2	teaspoons freshly ground black pepper, *McCormick®*
1	teaspoon or more cayenne, *McCormick®*
1	bottle (12-ounce) buffalo wing sauce, *Frank's Red Hot®*
	Blue cheese dressing, *Bob's Big Boy®*
	Celery sticks (optional)

1. Remove thin membrane from the back of ribs. Rub ribs with cut lemon; set aside.

2. In a small bowl, combine buffalo wing mix, garlic powder, black pepper, and cayenne. Sprinkle seasoning over ribs and pat in. Cover ribs with plastic wrap. Chill in refrigerator for 1 to 3 hours.

3. Soak 2 cups hickory wood chips in water for at least 1 hour. Set up grill for indirect cooking over medium heat (no heat source under ribs; see page 15). Let ribs stand at room temperature for 30 minutes.

4. Drain wood chips. Add some of the soaked wood chips to the smoke box if using a gas grill or place chips on hot coals if using charcoal. Place ribs on rib rack on hot grill over drip pan (or place ribs, bone sides down, directly on hot grill over drip pan). Cover grill. Cook for 2 to 2½ hours. Rotate ribs around rack every 30 minutes. If using charcoal, add 10 briquettes and a handful of soaked wood chips to each pile of coals every hour. If using a gas grill, add a handful of soaked wood chips to the smoke box every hour.

5. About 20 minutes before ribs are done, remove ribs from rib rack and place, meat sides down, on grill. Generously brush with wing sauce; stack ribs over the drip pan. Cover and cook for 10 minutes. Turn ribs; brush with additional wing sauce and restack. Cook 10 minutes more or until tender. Remove from grill; cut into portion sizes.

6. Serve hot with extra wing sauce, blue cheese dressing, and celery sticks (optional).

INDOOR METHOD:
Prepare ribs as directed. Preheat oven to 350 degrees F. Place ribs, bone sides down, on a wire rack in a shallow roasting pan. Cover tightly with aluminum foil. Bake in oven for 1 hour. Remove ribs from oven and carefully drain fat from roasting pan. Continue baking ribs, uncovered, for 30 to 45 minutes more or until tender, turning and brushing occasionally with wing sauce during the last 20 minutes of cooking. Serve as directed.

Smoked Spareribs with Backwoods BBQ Sauce

Prep 15 minutes
Grill 2½ hours
Makes 4 servings

2	racks pork spareribs
1	recipe All-Purpose Pork Rub (see page 65)

FOR BACKWOODS BBQ SAUCE:

1	bottle (12-ounce) chili sauce, *Heinz*®
1	can (12-ounce) cola, *Coca Cola*®
¼	cup Worcestershire sauce, *Lea & Perrins*®
¼	cup steak sauce, *A.1.*®
¼	teaspoon liquid smoke, *Wright's*®

1. Soak 2 cups hickory wood chips in water for at least 1 hour. Remove thin membrane from the backs of ribs. Pat All-Purpose Pork Rub onto all sides of ribs, using all of the rub. Set aside.

2. Set up grill for indirect cooking over medium heat (no heat source under ribs; see page 15). Drain wood chips. Add some of the soaked wood chips to the smoke box if using gas grill or place chips on hot coals if using charcoal.

3. Place ribs in rib rack on hot grill over drip pan (or place ribs, bone sides down, directly on hot grill over drip pan). Cover grill and cook 2½ to 3 hours or until ribs are tender. If using charcoal, add 10 briquettes and a handful of soaked wood chips to coals every hour. For gas grill, add some wood chips to the smoke box every hour.

4. For Backwoods BBQ Sauce, in a medium saucepan, combine chili sauce, cola, Worcestershire sauce, steak sauce, and liquid smoke. Cook over medium heat for 15 minutes. Remove from heat; set aside.

5. About 20 minutes before ribs are done, remove ribs from rib rack and place, meat sides down, on grill. Generously brush with Backwoods BBQ Sauce; stack ribs over drip pan. Cover and cook for 10 minutes. Turn ribs; brush with additional sauce and restack. Cook 10 minutes more or until tender. Transfer cooked ribs to platter and cut into portion sizes. Serve hot with remaining sauce.

INDOOR METHOD:
Prepare and rub ribs as directed. Preheat oven to 350 degrees F. Place ribs, bone sides down, on a rack in a shallow roasting pan. Cover tightly with aluminum foil. Bake in oven for 1 hour. Meanwhile, make Backwoods BBQ Sauce as directed. Remove ribs from oven and carefully drain fat from roasting pan. Continue baking ribs, uncovered, for 30 to 45 minutes more or until tender, turning and brushing occasionally with sauce during the last 20 minutes of cooking. Serve as directed.

Rosemary-Smoked Lamb Loin Chops

Prep 10 minutes **Grill** 16 minutes
Stand 25 minutes **Marinate** 3 hours
Makes 4 servings

8	lamb loin chops, 1½ to 2 inches thick
1	package (0.66-ounce) fresh rosemary
1	cup red wine
2	teaspoons herbes de Provence, *McCormick®*
2	teaspoons Montreal steak seasoning, *McCormick® Grill Mates®*
1	teaspoon crushed garlic, *Gourmet Garden®*

1. Place chops in a large zip-top bag; set aside. Coarsely chop 2 tablespoons of the rosemary, reserving stems. For marinade, in a small bowl, combine 1 tablespoon of the chopped rosemary, the wine, herbes de Provence, steak seasoning, and garlic. Pour into bag with lamb. Squeeze air out of bag; seal. Gently massage bag to coat lamb. Marinate in refrigerator for 3 to 6 hours.

2. In a small bowl, soak remaining rosemary and reserved stems in water until ready to cook. Set up grill for direct cooking over medium-high heat (see page 15). Oil grate when ready to start cooking. Remove lamb from marinade; discard marinade. Let lamb stand at room temperature for 20 minutes.

3. Drain rosemary and place on hot coals or in smoke box. Place chops on hot, oiled grill. Cover grill. Cook for 8 to 10 minutes per side for medium (135 to 140 degrees F). Let stand for 5 minutes. Serve hot. Sprinkle with the remaining 1 tablespoon chopped rosemary.

INDOOR METHOD:
Prepare and marinate chops as directed. Remove chops from marinade and discard marinade. Pat chops dry with paper towels. Place soaked rosemary on foil-lined baking sheet or broiler pan; place chops on top of rosemary. Broil 4 to 6 inches from the heat source for 4 to 8 minutes per side for medium (135 to 140 degrees F). Let stand for 5 minutes. Serve as directed.

Spatchcooked Leg of Lamb with Tandoori Spices

Prep 15 minutes   Grill 50 minutes
Stand 35 minutes   Marinate 4 hours
Makes 6 servings

Spatchcooking, or butterflying, shortens the grill time of this Indian favorite. Marinated in yogurt seasoned with ginger and garam masala, it gets its fiery color and taste from paprika and red pepper. The aromatic tandoori rub works equally well on chicken, salmon, or shrimp.

3½	pounds boneless leg of lamb
1½	cups plain yogurt, *Dannon*®
2	tablespoons soy sauce, *Kikkoman*®
1	tablespoon lemon juice, *Minute Maid*®
2	teaspoons garam masala,* *Spice Hunter*®
2	teaspoons paprika, *McCormick*®
2	teaspoons minced ginger, *Gourmet Garden*®
1	teaspoon crushed garlic, *Gourmet Garden*®
1	teaspoon red and black pepper blend, *McCormick*®

1. Remove netting from lamb, if present. Lay lamb on cutting board, opened up. With a sharp knife, butterfly open parts of meat that are more than 1 inch thick (see photo, page 9). Place in shallow baking pan; set aside.

2. In a medium bowl, combine yogurt, soy sauce, lemon juice, garam masala, paprika, ginger, garlic, and pepper blend, stirring until smooth. Pour over lamb, making sure it is thoroughly coated. Cover with plastic wrap; marinate in the refrigerator for 4 to 6 hours, preferably overnight.

3. Set up grill for indirect cooking over medium-high heat (no heat source directly under lamb; see page 15). Oil grate when ready to start cooking. Remove lamb from marinade; discard marinade. Crisscross 2 metal skewers through meat. Let stand at room temperature for 30 minutes.

4. Place lamb on hot, oiled grill over drip pan. Cover grill. Cook for 50 to 60 minutes for medium (150 degrees F). Remove from grill and let stand 5 to 10 minutes before slicing.

*NOTE: Garam masala is a blend of aromatic spices used in Indian cooking. It can be found in the spice section of the grocery store.

INDOOR METHOD:
Prepare lamb as directed. Preheat oven to 400 degrees F. Place on foil-lined baking sheet. Roast in oven for 50 to 60 minutes for medium (150 degrees F). Serve as directed.

Ginger-Glazed Rack of Lamb

Prep 10 minutes Grill 20 minutes
Stand 25 minutes Marinate 4 hours
Makes 6 servings

2 French-style lamb rib roasts

FOR SHERRY MARINADE:
1 cup ginger ale, *Canada Dry*®
½ cup dry sherry, *Christian Brothers*®
¼ cup soy sauce, *Kikkoman*®
1 tablespoon Szechwan seasoning, *McCormick*®
2 teaspoons minced ginger, *Gourmet Garden*®
1 teaspoon crushed garlic, *Gourmet Garden*®

FOR GINGER GLAZE:
¾ cup ginger preserves, *Robertson's*®
2 tablespoons dry sherry, *Christian Brothers*®
1 teaspoon Szechwan seasoning, *McCormick*®

1. Place lamb in large zip-top bag. For Sherry Marinade, in a medium bowl, stir together ginger ale, the ½ cup sherry, the soy sauce, the 1 tablespoon Szechwan seasoning, the ginger, and garlic. Pour into zip-top bag with lamb. Squeeze air out of bag; seal. Gently massage bag to coat lamb. Marinate in refrigerator for 4 to 6 hours.

2. Set up grill for direct cooking over medium-high heat (see page 15). Oil grate when ready to start cooking.

3. For Ginger Glaze, in a small saucepan, combine preserves, the 2 tablespoons sherry, and the 1 teaspoon Szechwan seasoning. Heat over medium heat, stirring until preserves have melted. Simmer for 5 minutes. Remove from heat; cool.

4. Remove lamb from marinade; discard marinade. Let lamb stand at room temperature for 20 minutes. Place lamb, meat sides down, on hot, oiled grill. Cook for 10 to 12 minutes. Turn and brush lamb with ginger glaze. Continue cooking for 10 to 12 minutes more for medium (135 to 140 degrees F),* basting with glaze every 5 minutes.

5. Remove from grill; let stand for 5 minutes. Meanwhile, reheat glaze to boiling. Brush lamb with hot glaze; cut lamb into portion-size chops. Serve cut chops with hot glaze.

*TIP: If bones start to burn on the grill, fold pieces of aluminum foil over the ends.

INDOOR METHOD:
Preheat oven to 425 degrees F. Prepare lamb as directed. Place, meat sides down, in foil-lined baking pan. Roast in oven for 20 to 30 minutes for medium (135 to 140 degrees F). Brush with glaze every 10 minutes. Transfer lamb to cutting board and tent with foil. Let stand for 10 minutes. Meanwhile, reheat glaze to boiling. Brush lamb with hot glaze. Serve as directed.

Things to Do with Your Turkey Fryer

Cajun cookin' has gone mainstream, and look no further than deep-fried turkey for proof of that. Deep frying is a real timesaver, getting your main course from pot to table in as little as 20 minutes, while delivering a unique flavor contrast—scrumptiously blackened on the outside; juicy on the inside.

Plus, when you have the turkey fryer heated up, you can use my Spicy Beer Batter to create melt-in-your-mouth appetizers and sides. Customize the batter to your taste by adding hot sauce or other seasonings, then use it to coat shrimp, pieces of fish or chicken, or cut-up vegetables such as onion rings, zucchini slices, cauliflower, or mushrooms. Fry these tidbits up to a crunchy golden brown in the turkey fryer and serve them to tide guests over until the main attraction is ready to be served.

The Recipes

Spicy Beer Batter

Prep 10 minutes   **Makes** about 3 cups

    2   eggs
    1   teaspoon paprika, *McCormick®*
    2   cups baking mix, *Bisquick®*
    1   cup ale, *Bass®*
         Shrimp, fish, chicken, and/or vegetables

1. In a large bowl, combine eggs and paprika. Stir in baking mix and ale.* Lightly flour shrimp or other food items. Dip in beer batter; fry in peanut oil heated to 375 degrees F until golden brown.

*TIP: For additional flavor, add a few drops of bottled hot pepper sauce (*Tabasco®*) or Buffalo hot wing sauce, or stir in 2 to 3 tablespoons of any marinade mix (*McCormick® Grill Mates®*).

Cajun Deep-Fried Turkey

Prep 30 minutes   **Cook** 36 minutes
Stand 10 minutes   **Makes** 12 servings

1   12-pound fresh or frozen turkey, thawed

FOR INJECTOR SAUCE:
1   cup reduced-sodium chicken broth, *Swanson*®
½   cup (1 stick) butter, melted
½   cup lemon juice, *Minute Maid*®
2   tablespoons Cajun seasoning, *McCormick*®
2   tablespoons garlic juice, *McCormick*®
½   teaspoon hot pepper sauce, *Tabasco*®

FOR RUB:
2   tablespoons Cajun seasoning, *McCormick*®
2   tablespoons paprika, *McCormick*®
1   tablespoon granulated garlic
1   tablespoon salt-free lemon-pepper seasoning, *McCormick*®

3   to 4 gallons peanut oil

1. Remove neck and giblets from turkey. Rinse the turkey body cavity; pat dry with paper towels. If present, remove and discard plastic leg holder and pop-up timer. Tuck ends of the drumsticks under band of skin across the tail or tie legs with butcher's string. Twist wing tips under back.

2. For Injector Sauce, in a bowl, whisk together chicken broth, butter, lemon juice, 2 tablespoons Cajun seasoning, the garlic juice, and hot pepper sauce. When ready to inject the turkey, strain the sauce through a fine-mesh strainer. For rub, in a bowl, combine 2 tablespoons Cajun seasoning, the paprika, granulated garlic, and lemon-pepper seasoning.

3. To prepare the turkey fryer, set up fryer according to manufacturer's instructions.* Add oil.** Preheat oil to 350 degrees F. Turn off fryer. Use a flavor-injector syringe to inject strained sauce into both sides of the turkey breast, each thigh, and each drumstick. Sprinkle rub over the entire surface of turkey and inside the cavity. Lower turkey into hot oil. Restart fryer; fry at 350 degrees F for 3 minutes per pound (about 36 minutes total). Carefully remove turkey from hot oil to check doneness: Insert an instant-read meat thermometer into the meaty part of a thigh. Turkey is done when thermometer registers 180 degrees F. If more time is needed, carefully lower the turkey back into oil and check again in 3 to 5 minutes.

4. When done, lift the turkey from the oil, allowing excess oil to drain back into the pot. Drain on wire rack. Let stand for 10 minutes before carving.

*TIP: Position fryer on a level dirt or concrete area with 10 feet of clearance all around. Wear oven mitts, apron, and goggles when using the fryer.

**NOTE: To determine how much oil is needed for frying, remove frying pot from unit. Place turkey in frying basket; lower into frying pot. Add enough water to cover turkey. Lift the turkey from pot, allowing excess water to drain into pot. Mark the water line. Drain water from pot; dry thoroughly. Fill pot to the marked line with peanut oil. Insert a deep-fat frying thermometer into the pot. Heat as directed.

Beer-'n'-Butter Deep-Fried Turkey

Prep 30 minutes   **Cook** 36 minutes
Stand 10 minutes   **Makes** 12 servings

1   **12-pound fresh or frozen turkey, thawed**

FOR INJECTOR SAUCE:
1   **cup ale, *Bass*®**
½   **cup (1 stick) butter, melted**
½   **cup lemon juice, *Minute Maid*®**
2   **tablespoons Italian herb marinade mix, *Durkee*® *Grill Creations*®**
2   **tablespoons garlic juice, *McCormick*®**

3   **to 4 gallons peanut oil**
       Salt
       Ground black pepper, *McCormick*®

1. Remove neck and giblets from turkey. Rinse the turkey body cavity; pat dry with paper towels. If present, remove and discard plastic leg holder and pop-up timer. Tuck ends of the drumsticks under band of skin across the tail or tie legs to tail with butcher's string. Twist wing tips under back.

2. For Injector Sauce, in a medium bowl, whisk together ale, butter, lemon juice, marinade mix, and garlic juice. When ready to inject the turkey, strain the sauce through a fine-mesh strainer.

3. To prepare the turkey fryer, set up fryer according to manufacturer's instructions (see tip, page 88). Add oil (see note, page 88). Preheat oil to 350 degrees F. Turn off fryer. Use a flavor-injector syringe to inject strained sauce into both sides of the turkey breast, each thigh, and each drumstick. Season with salt and pepper.

4. Lower turkey into hot oil. Restart fryer and fry at 350 degrees F for 3 minutes per pound (about 36 minutes total). Carefully remove turkey from hot oil to check doneness: Insert an instant-read meat thermometer into the meaty part of a thigh. Turkey is done when thermometer registers 180 degrees F. If more time is needed, carefully lower the turkey back into oil and check again in 3 to 5 minutes.

5. When ready, carefully lift the turkey from the oil, allowing excess oil to drain back into the pot. Drain on wire rack. Let stand for 10 to 15 minutes before carving.

Grand Marnier® Chicken

Prep 20 minutes **Cook** 20 minutes
Stand 10 minutes **Makes** 6 servings

1	4-pound whole roasting chicken

FOR INJECTOR SAUCE:

⅓	cup *Grand Marnier*®
⅓	cup frozen limeade concentrate, thawed, *Minute Maid*®
¼	cup soy sauce, *Kikkoman*®
¼	cup (½ stick) butter, melted
1	tablespoon chile-garlic sauce, *Lee Kum Kee*®
1	tablespoon frozen orange juice concentrate, thawed, *Minute Maid*®
1	tablespoon minced ginger, *Gourmet Garden*®

2	gallons peanut oil

1. Remove the giblets and neck from chicken. Rinse chicken body cavity; pat dry with paper towels. Skewer neck skin to back. Tie legs to tail with butcher's string. Twist wings under the back; set aside.

2. For Injector Sauce, in a medium bowl, whisk together Grand Marnier®, limeade concentrate, soy sauce, butter, chile-garlic sauce, orange juice concentrate, and ginger. When ready to inject the turkey, strain the sauce through a fine-mesh strainer.

3. To prepare the turkey fryer, set up fryer according to manufacturer's instructions (see tip, page 88). Add oil to pot. Insert deep-fat frying thermometer into the pot and preheat oil to 350 degrees F. Turn off fryer. Use a flavor-injector syringe to inject strained sauce into both sides of the breast, each thigh, and each drumstick.

4. Place chicken, breast side up, in frying basket. Slowly lower basket into the hot oil. Restart the fryer and fry at 350 degrees F for 5 to 7 minutes per pound (about 20 minutes total). Carefully remove chicken from hot oil to check doneness: Insert an instant-read meat thermometer into meaty part of thigh. Chicken is done when thermometer registers 180 degrees F. If more time is needed, carefully lower the chicken back into the oil and check again in 3 to 5 minutes.

5. When ready, carefully lift the chicken from the oil, allowing excess oil to drain back into the pot. Drain on wire rack. Let stand for 10 to 15 minutes before carving.

Apple and Jack Deep-Fried Pork Roast

Prep 30 minutes Cook 48 minutes
Stand 10 minutes Makes 6 servings

1	**6-pound boneless pork shoulder roast**

FOR INJECTOR SAUCE:

½	**cup (1 stick) butter**
⅓	**cup whiskey, *Jack Daniel's*®**
⅓	**cup apple cider, *Tree Top*®**
2	**tablespoons packed brown sugar, *C&H*®**
1	**tablespoon garlic juice, *McCormick*®**
2	**teaspoons seafood seasoning, *Old Bay*®**

2	**gallons peanut oil**

1. Tie pork roast together with butcher's string so that it is of uniform thickness to promote even cooking.

2. For Injector Sauce, in a medium saucepan, combine butter, whiskey, cider, brown sugar, garlic juice, and seafood seasoning. Simmer over medium heat until butter is melted and sugar is dissolved. When ready to inject the roast, strain the injector sauce through a fine-mesh strainer.

3. To prepare the turkey fryer, set up fryer according to the manufacturer's instructions (see tip, page 88). Add oil to pot. Insert deep-fat frying thermometer into the pot and preheat oil to 350 degrees F. Turn off fryer. Use a flavor-injector syringe to inject strained sauce into several spots on the roast.

4. Place roast in fryer basket. Slowly lower roast into hot oil. Restart fryer and fry at 350 degrees F for 8 minutes per pound (about 48 minutes total). Carefully remove roast from hot oil to check doneness. Insert an instant-read meat thermometer into roast. Roast is done when thermometer registers 150 degrees F. If more time is needed, carefully lower roast back into oil and check again in 3 to 5 minutes.

5. When ready, carefully lift roast from the oil, allowing excess oil to drain back into the pot. Drain on wire rack. Let roast stand for 10 to 15 minutes before slicing.

Deep-Fried Prime Rib with Madeira Sauce

Prep 20 minutes **Cook** 15 minutes
Stand 15 minutes **Marinate** 8 hours
Makes 6 servings

1	**3-pound boneless beef rib roast**
12	**whole peeled garlic cloves, *Global Farms*®**
1	**can (14-ounce) lower-sodium beef broth, *Swanson*®**
2	**tablespoons chopped fresh rosemary**
1	**tablespoon garlic juice, *McCormick*®**
1	**packet (1.1-ounce) beefy onion soup mix, *Lipton*®**
¾	**cup Madeira, *Paul Masson*®**
2	**tablespoons rosemary olive oil, *Boyajian*®**
2	**gallons peanut oil**

1. Roll and tie roast with butcher's string, if not already done. Using the tip of a small knife, poke 12 holes into the roast. Insert garlic cloves into holes; set aside.

2. In a medium saucepan, combine beef broth, rosemary, garlic juice and soup mix. Bring to a boil. Remove from heat and cool.

3. For marinade, in a medium bowl, combine 1⅓ cups of the beef broth mixture, ¼ cup of the Madeira, and the rosemary oil. Place roast in a large zip-top bag and pour in marinade. Press air out of bag; seal. Gently massage bag to coat roast. Marinate in refrigerator for 8 to 24 hours. Cover remaining beef broth mixture and chill until ready to use.

4. Remove roast from zip-top bag; reserve marinade. Strain reserved beef broth mixture (not marinade) through a fine-mesh strainer. Use flavor-injector syringe to inject strained mixture into several places on the roast.

5. For Madeira Sauce, pour the remaining ½ cup Madeira into a saucepan. Bring to a boil; cook over medium-high heat until reduced to ¼ cup. Add reserved marinade and boil for 5 minutes. Remove from heat. Reheat when ready to serve.

6. To prepare turkey fryer, set up fryer according to manufacturer's instructions (see tip, page 88). Add oil to pot. Insert deep-fat frying thermometer into the pot and preheat oil to 350 degrees F. Turn off fryer.

7. Lower roast into hot oil. Restart fryer and fry at 350 degrees F for 5 minutes per pound (about 15 minutes total). Carefully remove roast from hot oil to check doneness: Insert an instant-read meat thermometer into the roast. Roast is done when thermometer registers 140 degrees F. If more time is needed, carefully lower the roast back into oil and check again in 3 to 5 minutes.

8. When roast is done, carefully lift the roast from the oil, allowing excess oil to drain back into the pot. Drain on wire rack. Let stand for 15 minutes before slicing. Serve hot with Madeira Sauce.

Deep-Fried Whole Snapper

Prep 15 minutes **Cook** 3 minutes
Marinate 30 minutes **Makes** 4 servings

4	small whole snapper, cleaned and heads removed
⅓	cup light rum, *Bacardi®*
3	tablespoons canola oil, *Wesson®*
3	tablespoons lime juice, *ReaLime®*
1	package (1.06-ounce) herb marinade mix, *McCormick® Grill Mates®*
2	teaspoons chili powder, *Gebhardt's®*
2	gallons peanut oil

1. Score sides of fish 4 times. Place in a 13×9-inch baking dish. In a bowl, whisk together rum, canola oil, lime juice, marinade mix, and chili powder. Pour over fish. Turn fish over to coat. Cover with plastic wrap. Marinate in refrigerator for 30 minutes to 2 hours.

2. Set up fryer according to manufacturer's instructions (see tip, page 88). Add oil to pot. Insert deep-fat frying thermometer into pot; preheat oil to 350 degrees F. Turn off fryer. Remove fish from marinade; discard marinade. Pat fish dry, inside and out. Using a frying basket, lower the fish into the hot oil. Restart fryer; fry at 350 degrees F for 3 to 5 minutes or until golden brown and fish flakes easily. Carefully lift the fish from the oil, allowing the excess oil to drain into pot. Place on wire rack. Serve with *tortillas, lime wedges, cilantro,* and/or *chopped onions* (optional).

Slash-and-Fry Trout

Prep 10 minutes **Cook** 3 minutes
Marinate 30 minutes **Makes** 4 servings

4	whole trout, cleaned and heads removed
1	cup pineapple juice, *Dole®*
¼	cup soy sauce, *Kikkoman®*
1	tablespoon salt-free Thai seasoning, *Spice Hunter®*
1	to 2 gallons peanut oil
1	box (8-ounce) tempura batter mix, *Dynasty®*
½	cup fresh basil leaves, torn
½	cup fresh mint leaves, torn
¼	cup fresh cilantro leaves
1	jar (4-ounce) chopped pimiento, drained, *Dromedary®*
2	scallions (green onions), sliced diagonally
1	tablespoon seasoned rice vinegar, *Marukan®*

1. Score sides of trout 4 times. Place in a large zip-top bag. Add pineapple juice, soy sauce, and Thai seasoning. Massage bag. Squeeze air out of bag; seal. Marinate in refrigerator for 30 minutes to 2 hours.

2. Set up fryer according to manufacturer's instructions (see tip, page 88). Add oil to pot. Insert deep-fat frying thermometer into the pot; preheat oil to 350 degrees F. Turn off fryer. Remove trout from marinade; discard marinade. Pat dry. Dredge fish inside and out in batter mixture. Shake off excess. Using a frying basket, lower the trout into the hot oil. Restart fryer; fry at 350 degrees F for 3 to 5 minutes or until fish flakes easily. Carefully lift the trout from the oil, allowing excess oil to drain into pot. Place on wire rack. For herb salad, toss together basil, mint, cilantro, pimiento, scallions, and rice vinegar. Serve trout hot with herb salad.

New England Clambake

Prep 30 minutes
Cook 40 minutes
Makes 6 servings

A traditional clambake takes all day and requires digging a sand pit. This version delivers the same fun for a lot less work! Lobster, steamers, mussels, and heaps of corn and potatoes are wrapped in packets and steamed to buttery bliss in a basket at the bottom of the deep fryer.

½	cup (1 stick) butter, softened
2	tablespoons seafood seasoning, *Old Bay*®
6	lobster tails
3	pounds steamer clams, cleaned
3	pounds mussels, cleaned and debearded
1½	packages (4 count each) cleaned and cut prepackaged corn on the cob (6 total), *Green Giant*®
12	assorted small red, yellow, and purple creamer potatoes, quartered
2	large sweet onions, quartered
12	sprigs fresh thyme
6	whole cloves garlic, smashed
	Chopped fresh flat-leaf parsley (optional)
	Lemon wedges

1. In a small bowl, stir together butter and seafood seasoning until well mixed. Cover with plastic wrap and refrigerate until ready to use.

2. Tear six 18-inch squares of aluminum foil. Cut six 18-inch squares of 100%-cotton cheesecloth. Top each foil square with a piece of cheesecloth. Divide lobster, clams, mussels, corn, potatoes, onions, thyme, and garlic among cheesecloth squares, placing ingredients in the center of each cheesecloth square. Spoon a heaping tablespoon of the butter mixture on top of each serving. Gather each corner of cheesecloth to the middle and twist at top. Gather each corner of the foil to the middle and fold over securely.

3. Place steaming basket or rack in the bottom of a turkey fryer. Fill with water until it almost reaches the bottom of the basket. Start turkey fryer and bring water to a boil. Reduce heat, but maintain a constant boil. Stack foil packets on steamer basket. Cover top of fryer with additional aluminum foil and close lid.

4. Steam for 40 minutes, checking periodically to be sure the pot does not boil dry and adding hot water as needed. Using tongs, remove lid and carefully remove foil packets. Transfer packets to serving plates. Open packets carefully and top with chopped parsley (optional). Serve immediately with lemon wedges.

Southern Crawfish Boil

Prep 20 minutes
Cook 20 minutes
Makes 10 servings

Crawfish look like little lobsters, boiled live in the shell with Cajun spices. Buy the premixed bag seasoning—it drops right in the pot to save time. To serve them Louisiana-style, pour the drained crawfish on a newspaper-covered table and serve with hot sauce to make them super spicy.

2	boxes (3 ounces each) crab boil in bag, *Zatarain's*®
3	pounds small red potatoes
3	large sweet onions, quartered
4	lemons, sliced
7	pounds crawfish in shell, cleaned
2	packages (6 count each) frozen corn on the cob (12 total), thawed, *Green Giant*®
1	bottle (4-ounce) concentrated shrimp and crab boil, *Zatarain's*® Louisiana-style hot sauce, *Crystal*®

1. Fill turkey fryer with water to maximum fill line. Add crab boil bags. Start turkey fryer and bring water to a boil. Remove crab boil bags and set aside.

2. Place potatoes and onions in the bottom of frying basket. Lower basket into boiling water. Return crab boil bags to pot. Add lemons to water around the basket and cover with lid. Boil for 10 to 15 minutes or until potatoes are tender, but not fully cooked.

3. Add crawfish, corn, shrimp, and the crab boil concentrate. Boil for 10 to 15 minutes more or until crawfish are cooked through.

4. Remove lid and carefully lift basket out of water; drain. Scatter onto a butcher paper-covered picnic table or transfer to a large serving platter. Serve immediately with some of the crawfish boiling liquid and Louisiana-style hot sauce.

Gumbo for a Crowd

Start to Finish 1¾ hours
Makes 25 servings

3	pounds boneless, skinless chicken breast halves
3	pounds boneless, skinless chicken thighs
2	tablespoons Cajun seasoning, *McCormick®*
2	tablespoons or more vegetable oil, *Wesson®*
1	cup (2 sticks) butter
6	bags (12 ounces each) frozen seasoning blend (chopped onions, peppers, celery) thawed, *Pictsweet®*
2	bags (16 ounces each) frozen cut okra, thawed, *Pictsweet®*
2	tablespoons crushed garlic, *Gourmet Garden®*
3	packages (12 ounces each) beef hot links, cut into ¼-inch-thick rounds, *Hillshire Farm®*
2	packages (16 ounces each) beef smoked sausages, cut into ¼-inch-thick rounds, *Hillshire Farm®*
6	cans (49 ounces each) reduced-sodium chicken broth, *Swanson®*
6	cups water
4	boxes (7 ounces each) gumbo mix with rice, *Zatarain's®*
3	bay leaves
4	pounds frozen peeled and deveined large shrimp, thawed
6	pounds frozen crab legs, thawed
	Salt
	Ground black pepper, *McCormick®*
¼	cup gumbo filé powder,* *Zatarain's®*
	Hot cooked white rice
	Louisiana-style hot sauce, *Crystal®*

1. Cut chicken into bite-size pieces. In a large bowl, toss chicken with Cajun seasoning. In a large, deep skillet, heat oil over medium heat. Brown chicken, working in batches if necessary. Remove from skillet; set aside.

2. Wipe out skillet and return to heat. Melt butter in skillet. Add seasoning blend, okra, and garlic. Cook until completely heated through, stirring frequently. Remove from heat and set aside.

3. Set a 30- to 34-quart turkey fryer on medium heat. Add hot links and sausage to fryer. Cook, stirring occasionally, until lightly brown and juices are released. Add chicken and vegetable mixture and stir to mix.

4. Add chicken broth, the water, gumbo mix, and bay leaves. Stir to thoroughly combine. Simmer for 1 hour. Add the shrimp and crab legs and simmer about 15 minutes more or until shrimp and crab are cooked through. During the last 5 minutes of cooking, check seasoning and adjust with salt and pepper. Stir in filé powder. Serve hot with rice and Louisiana-style hot sauce.

*TIP: Filé powder is made from ground, dried leaves of the sassafras tree. It has become an integral part of Creole cooking and is used to thicken and flavor gumbos and other Creole dishes. Filé powder can be found in the spice section of the supermarket.

Beef

You don't need an expensive cut of meat to get a great meal. All you need is a great sauce and a grill. It'd be a shame to limit yourself to just one sauce, so this chapter serves up 14! These big-flavor sauces and melt-in-your-mouth marinades tenderize even the toughest meats, while locking in juices that taste wonderfully complex.

And if you think you've tried all the best barbecue sauces before, you need to give my All-Purpose Beef BBQ Sauce a try! It brings a depth of flavor to anything—from steak to ribs—by mixing thick, sweet molasses and tart vinegar into a robust sauce that cooks up quick and delicious. Or try it on burgers, chicken, or pork for variety. Big flavors and endless possibilities—that's what makes barbecuing fun!

The Recipes

All-Purpose Beef BBQ Sauce

Prep 5 minutes   **Cook** 10 minutes   **Makes** 2¾ cups

- 1   bottle (12-ounce) chili sauce, *Heinz*®
- ½   cup coffee liqueur, *Kahlúa*®
- ⅓   cup molasses, *Grandma's*®
- ¼   cup cider vinegar, *Heinz*®
- 1   packet (1.1-ounce) beefy onion soup mix, *Lipton*®
- 2   tablespoons ground black pepper, *McCormick*®

1. In a medium saucepan, stir to combine chili sauce, coffee liqueur, molasses, vinegar, soup mix, and pepper over medium heat. Simmer for 10 minutes. Remove from heat and cool. Cover and store in the refrigerator for up to 1 week.

Sandra at her alma mater homecoming game (left).

Red Wine T-Bone Steaks

Prep 40 minutes   Grill 10 minutes
Stand 25 minutes   Marinate 2 hours
Makes 4 servings

4	¾-inch-thick beef T-bone steaks
1½	cups red wine
4½	teaspoons salt-free garlic-herb seasoning, *McCormick®*
1	tablespoon Montreal steak seasoning, *McCormick® Grill Mates®*

FOR RED WINE BUTTER:

1	cup red wine
⅓	cup finely chopped shallots
1	tablespoon frozen orange juice concentrate, *Minute Maid®*
1	teaspoon crushed garlic, finely chopped, *Gourmet Garden®*
½	cup (1 stick) butter, softened

INDOOR METHOD:

Prepare steaks and Red Wine Butter as directed. Preheat broiler. Remove steaks from marinade; discard marinade. Place steaks on foil-lined baking sheet or broiler pan. Broil 6 to 8 inches from heat source for 5 minutes; turn and broil for 4 minutes more for medium (160 degrees F). Serve as directed.

1. Place steaks in large zip-top bag. Add the 1½ cups wine, the garlic-herb seasoning, and steak seasoning. Squeeze air out of bag; seal. Gently massage bag to combine. Marinate in refrigerator for 2 to 4 hours.

2. For Red Wine Butter, in a saucepan, combine the 1 cup wine, the shallots, orange juice concentrate, and garlic. Reduce mixture over medium-high heat to ¼ cup; cool completely. Work reduction into butter with a fork; form into a log. Wrap with plastic wrap. Chill until firm.

3. Set up grill for direct cooking over high heat (see page 15). Oil grate when ready to start cooking. Let steaks stand at room temperature for 20 to 30 minutes. Remove steaks from marinade; discard marinade. Place steaks on hot, oiled grill and cook for 5 to 7 minutes per side for medium (160 degrees F). Transfer steaks to a platter; let stand for 5 minutes before serving. Serve with slices of Red Wine Butter.

Peppercorn Steaks

Prep 10 minutes   Grill 12 minutes
Stand 25 minutes   Marinate 2 hours
Makes 4 servings

New York Strip steak needs only a lightly seasoned oil-and-vinegar marinade and a sprinkle of rose-colored peppercorns to let the flavor shine through.

4	1-inch-thick New York beef strip steaks
1½	cups olive oil-and-vinegar salad dressing, *Newman's Own®*
¼	cup chopped fresh flat-leaf parsley
¼	cup pink peppercorns, *Spice Hunter®*
1	tablespoon Montreal steak seasoning, *McCormick® Grill Mates®*

INDOOR METHOD:

Preheat broiler. Prepare as directed. Remove steaks from marinade. Place steaks on foil-lined baking sheet. Broil 6 inches from heat for 5 minutes. Turn; broil 5 minutes more.

1. Place steaks in a large zip-top bag; add salad dressing, parsley, peppercorns, and steak seasoning. Squeeze air out of bag; seal. Gently massage bag to combine. Marinate in refrigerator for 2 to 4 hours.

2. Set up grill for direct cooking over high heat (see page 15). Oil grate when ready to start cooking. Let steaks stand at room temperature for 20 to 30 minutes. Remove steaks from marinade; discard marinade. Place steaks on hot, oiled grill and cook for 6 to 8 minutes per side for medium (160 degrees F). Let stand for 5 minutes before serving.

Rib Steaks with Raspberry-Tarragon Sauce

Prep 10 minutes **Grill** 10 minutes
Stand 25 minutes **Marinate** 2 hours
Makes 4 servings

4	¾-inch-thick beef ribeye steaks
⅓	cup canola oil, *Wesson*®
¼	cup red wine, *Pompeian*®
3	tablespoons steak sauce, *A.1.*®
2	tablespoons raspberry vinegar, *Kozlowski Farms*®
1	packet (0.7-ounce) Italian salad dressing mix, *Good Seasons*®

FOR RASPBERRY-TARRAGON SAUCE:

¼	cup butter
½	cup finely chopped shallots
¼	cup raspberry vinegar, *Kozlowski Farms*®
¼	cup finely chopped fresh tarragon
2	tablespoons steak sauce, *A.1.*®

1. Place steaks in large zip-top bag; add canola oil, wine, the 3 tablespoons steak sauce, the 2 tablespoons vinegar, and the salad dressing mix. Squeeze air out of bag and seal. Gently massage bag to combine. Marinate in refrigerator for 2 to 4 hours.

2. For Raspberry-Tarragon Sauce, in a small saucepan, melt butter. Add shallots and cook and stir until soft but not brown. Add the ¼ cup vinegar and simmer for 2 minutes. Remove from heat and stir in tarragon and the 2 tablespoons steak sauce. Set aside until ready to serve.

3. Set up grill for direct cooking over high heat (see page 15). Oil grate when ready to start cooking.

4. Let steaks stand at room temperature for 20 to 30 minutes. Remove steaks from marinade; discard marinade. Place steaks on hot, oiled grill and cook for 5 to 7 minutes per side for medium (160 degrees F).

5. Transfer steaks to a platter and let stand for 5 minutes before serving. Serve with Raspberry-Tarragon Sauce (reheat sauce if necessary).

INDOOR METHOD:
Prepare steaks and Raspberry-Tarragon Sauce as directed. Preheat broiler. Remove steaks from marinade; discard marinade. Place steaks on foil-lined baking sheet or broiler pan. Broil 6 to 8 inches from heat source for 5 minutes; turn and broil for 4 minutes more for medium (160 degrees F).

Planked Filet Mignons with Portobello Mushrooms

Prep 20 minutes   **Grill** 14 minutes
Stand 35 minutes   **Marinate** 2 hours
Makes 4 servings

2	**cups port wine**
2	**cups lower-sodium beef broth, _Swanson_®**
4	**8-ounce beef tenderloin steaks, cut 1 inch thick**
4	**slices bacon, _Oscar Mayer_®**
4	**4-inch portobello mushrooms**
1	**packet (1-ounce) au jus gravy mix, _McCormick_®**
2	**tablespoons balsamic vinegar**
1½	**tablespoons crushed garlic, _Gourmet Garden_®**
½	**cup chopped fresh herbs (such as thyme, rosemary, marjoram, parsley)**
	Rosemary sprig (optional)

1. Soak alder grilling plank in 1 cup of the port wine and 1 cup of the beef broth for at least 1 hour. Set aside until ready to grill.

2. Wrap each steak with one slice of bacon and secure with a wooden toothpick; place in a baking dish. Wipe mushrooms with a dry cloth (do not get wet). Remove and discard stems. Place caps in baking dish. In a small bowl, stir together remaining 1 cup port wine, the remaining 1 cup beef broth, gravy mix, vinegar, garlic, and chopped herbs. Pour over steaks and mushrooms in baking dish. Cover with plastic wrap. Marinate in refrigerator for 2 to 4 hours.

3. Set up grill for direct cooking over medium-high heat (see page 15). Oil grate when ready to start cooking. Remove steaks from refrigerator; let stand at room temperature about 30 minutes. Remove steaks and mushrooms from marinade; discard marinade. Season the plank by removing plank from wine-broth mixture and placing on hot, oiled grill. Cover and grill for 3 minutes. Plank may be warped; turn plank every minute until it flattens out.

4. Place steaks and mushrooms on plank and close the grill lid. Cook for 10 minutes. Turn the steaks and place a mushroom cap on top of each steak. Close lid; cook for 4 to 5 minutes more for medium-rare (145 degrees F). Remove steaks from grill; cover and let stand for 5 minutes. Serve either with the mushroom caps on top of or underneath the steaks. Garnish each with a rosemary sprig (optional).

INDOOR METHOD:
Omit alder plank. Prepare steaks and mushrooms as directed using 1 cup port wine and 1 cup beef broth. Preheat broiler. Place steaks and mushrooms (bottom sides up) on foil-lined baking sheet or broiler pan. Broil 6 to 8 inches from heat source for 6 to 8 minutes per side for medium-rare (145 degrees F). Remove from broiler. Cover and let stand for 5 minutes.

Chipotle Java-Rubbed Tenderloin

Prep 10 minutes   **Grill** 40 minutes
Stand 35 minutes   **Chill** 2 hours
Makes 4 servings

1½	pounds center-cut beef tenderloin roast, trimmed of fat and silver skin
1	packet (1.13-ounce) chipotle pepper marinade mix, *McCormick® Grill Mates®*
½	cup instant coffee crystals, *Folgers®*
½	teaspoon ground cinnamon, *McCormick®*

1. Tie tenderloin roast with butcher's string to hold roast together (tuck any thin ends under for a uniform thickness). In a small bowl, combine marinade mix, coffee crystals, and cinnamon. Rub into tenderloin. Wrap in plastic wrap; chill in refrigerator for 2 to 4 hours.

2. Set up grill for direct cooking over medium heat (see page 15). Oil grate when ready to start cooking. Let meat stand at room temperature for 30 to 40 minutes.

3. Place tenderloin on hot, oiled grill. Cook about 40 minutes for medium (150 degrees F), rolling roast a quarter turn every 10 minutes. Remove from grill; let stand for 5 to 10 minutes. Slice tenderloin in ½-inch-thick slices. Serve immediately.

INDOOR METHOD:
Preheat oven to 500 degrees F. Prepare tenderloin as directed. Place on rack in roasting pan and place in oven. Immediately reduce temperature to 400 degrees F. Roast for 30 to 35 minutes for medium (150 degrees F). Remove from oven and let stand for 5 to 10 minutes.

Tri-Tip Steak with Mango-Red Pepper Salsa

Prep 20 minutes **Grill** 1 hour
Stand 25 minutes **Marinate** 2 hours
Makes 4 servings

1 2½-pound beef tri-tip steak
1 can (11.5-ounce) mango nectar, *Kern's®*
½ cup chopped fresh cilantro
¼ cup diced canned jalapeño chile peppers, *Ortega®*
¼ cup lime juice, *ReaLime®*
¼ cup canola oil, *Wesson®*
1 tablespoon Jamaican jerk seasoning, *McCormick®*

FOR MANGO-RED PEPPER SALSA:
1 jar (12-ounce) roasted red bell peppers, diced fine, *Delallo®*
8 ounces frozen mango chunks, diced small, *Dole®*
¼ cup chopped fresh cilantro
2 tablespoons lime juice, *ReaLime®*
1 fresh jalapeño chile pepper, finely chopped (see note, page 23)
¼ teaspoon salt

1. Place steak in a large zip-top bag; add the mango nectar, the ½ cup cilantro, the canned chile peppers, the ¼ cup lime juice, canola oil, and the jerk seasoning. Squeeze air out of bag; seal. Gently massage bag to combine. Marinate in refrigerator for 2 to 4 hours.

2. For Mango-Red Pepper Salsa, in a medium bowl, combine roasted red bell peppers, mango, the ¼ cup cilantro, the 2 tablespoons lime juice, the fresh chile pepper, and the salt. Set aside until ready to serve.

3. Set up grill for indirect cooking over medium-high heat (no direct heat source under steak; see page 15). Oil grate when ready to start cooking. Let steak stand at room temperature for 20 to 30 minutes.

4. Remove steak from marinade; discard marinade. Place steak on hot, oiled grill. Cover grill and cook for 30 to 35 minutes per side for medium (145 to 150 degrees F).

5. Transfer steak to a platter and let stand for 5 to 10 minutes before thinly slicing across the grain. Serve warm with Mango-Red Pepper Salsa.

INDOOR METHOD:
Prepare steak and Mango-Red Pepper Salsa as directed. Preheat the oven to 450 degrees F. Remove steak from marinade; discard marinade. Place steak, fat side up, on a rack in a shallow roasting pan. Roast in oven about 30 minutes for medium (145 to 150 degrees F); tent with foil and let stand for 10 minutes. Serve as directed.

Southwestern Stuffed Flank Steak

Prep 25 minutes **Grill** 1 ½ hours
Stand 5 minutes **Makes** 4 servings

FOR SOUTHWESTERN RUB:

1 packet (1.25-ounce) chili seasoning mix, *McCormick®*
2 tablespoons packed brown sugar, *C&H®*
1 tablespoon paprika, *McCormick®*
1 teaspoon ground cinnamon, *McCormick®*

FOR STEAK:

1 1¾-pound beef flank steak
3 cups baby spinach, *Fresh Express®*
6 ounces thinly sliced prosciutto
½ package (24-ounce) polenta, cut in half lengthwise
1 cup roasted red bell peppers, cut into strips, *Delallo®*
1 can (7-ounce) diced roasted green chiles, *Ortega®*

1. For Southwestern Rub, in a small bowl, combine chili seasoning mix, brown sugar, paprika, and cinnamon. Set aside.

2. Place steak on cutting board and with a very sharp knife, butterfly steak, cutting horizontally through the meat lengthwise and leaving it hinged together on one side (see photo, page 9). Open steak and season with Southwestern Rub on both sides.

3. Place the steak on a piece of aluminum foil so the grain of the meat runs side-to-side and parallel to the edge of the counter. Starting at the edge nearest you, arrange spinach over steak, leaving 1 inch at the far end bare. Top spinach with prosciutto. Cut the polenta lengthwise into ½-inch-wide strips. Lay polenta strips across the prosciutto (with the grain of the steak), alternating with roasted red bell pepper strips. Sprinkle green chiles on top. Starting at the edge nearest you, roll the steak up like a jelly roll. Wrap the foil around the meat and twist the ends to secure.

4. Set up grill for indirect cooking over medium heat (no direct heat source under steak; see page 15). Place wrapped steak on hot grill and cover grill. Cook for 1 ½ to 2 hours or until internal temperature reaches 165 degrees F, turning every 20 minutes. Remove steak from grill. Let stand for 5 to 10 minutes before slicing.

INDOOR METHOD:
Preheat oven to 350 degrees F. Prepare steak as directed. Place wrapped steak in a roasting pan. Roast in oven for 1½ to 2 hours or until internal temperature reaches 165 degrees F. Serve as directed.

Thai Grilled Beef Salad

Prep 20 minutes   **Grill** 10 minutes
Stand 25 minutes   **Marinate** 1 hour
Makes 4 servings

1	1½-pound beef flank steak
¾	cup dry sherry, *Christian Brothers*®
¼	cup canola oil, *Wesson*®
¼	cup soy sauce, *Kikkoman*®
1	fresh red chile pepper, finely chopped (see note, page 23)
2	tablespoons Thai seasoning, *Spice Islands*®
2	tablespoons lime juice, *ReaLime*®

FOR SESAME SALAD DRESSING:

¼	cup soy sauce, *Kikkoman*®
3	tablespoons lime juice, *ReaLime*®
2	tablespoons sherry vinegar
2	tablespoons toasted sesame oil
1	tablespoon Thai seasoning, *Spice Island*®

FOR SALAD:

12	cups butter lettuce salad mix, *Fresh Express*®
16	cherry tomatoes, halved, *Nature Sweet*®
1	cucumber, sliced
	Chopped fresh cilantro (optional)
	Chopped fresh mint (optional)

1. Place steak in a large zip-top bag and add the sherry, canola oil, ¼ cup soy sauce, red chile, the 2 tablespoons Thai seasoning, and the 2 tablespoons lime juice. Squeeze air out of bag; seal. Gently massage bag to combine. Marinate in refrigerator for 1 to 3 hours.

2. For Sesame Salad Dressing, in a medium bowl, whisk together ¼ cup soy sauce, the 3 tablespoons lime juice, vinegar, sesame oil, and the 1 tablespoon Thai seasoning. Set aside until ready to serve.

3. Set up grill for direct cooking over high heat (see page 15). Oil grate when ready to start cooking. Let steak stand at room temperature for 20 to 30 minutes. Remove steak from marinade; discard marinade.

4. Place steak on hot, oiled grill and cook for 5 to 8 minutes per side for medium (160 degrees F). Transfer steak to a platter and let stand for 5 minutes before slicing thinly across the grain.

5. For salads, divide salad mix, tomatoes, and cucumber among four chilled plates. Arrange steak slices on top and drizzle with Sesame Salad Dressing. Top with chopped cilantro (optional) and mint (optional).

INDOOR METHOD:
Prepare steak and Sesame Salad Dressing as directed. Preheat broiler. Remove steak from marinade; discard marinade. Place steak on foil-lined pan. Broil 6 to 8 inches from heat source for 5 minutes; turn and broil for 4 to 5 minutes more for medium (160 degrees F). Serve salad as directed.

Churrasco Beef with Chimichurri

Prep 20 minutes
Grill 4 minutes
Makes 4 servings

This popular Argentinean dish is a mixture of Spanish and Italian favorites. Brazilian churrasco, or juicy tenderloin, is grilled hot and fast and served with a pesto-like chimichurri sauce of chopped parsley, oregano and garlic, intensified with red pepper and red wine vinaigrette.

1	1½-pound center-cut beef tenderloin roast, trimmed of fat and silver skin
2	tablespoons Montreal steak seasoning, *McCormick® Grill Mates®*
1	tablespoon Mexican oregano, *McCormick®*
½	teaspoon ground cumin, *McCormick®*

FOR CHIMICHURRI:

2	tablespoons crushed garlic, *Gourmet Garden®*
1	bunch fresh flat-leaf parsley
¼	cup fresh oregano
½	teaspoon red pepper flakes, *McCormick®*
¾	cup red wine vinaigrette, *Wish-Bone®*
¼	teaspoon salt

1. Place tenderloin on a cutting board. Holding your knife parallel to the cutting board, cut the tenderloin lengthwise with the grain into ½-inch-thick flat even slices. Place each slice between 2 sheets of plastic wrap and pound with a meat mallet to a thickness of ¼ inch. In a small bowl, combine steak seasoning, oregano, and cumin. Rub seasoning mixture into both sides of steak slices. Set aside.

2. For Chimichurri, in a food processor, combine garlic, parsley, oregano, and red pepper flakes. Cover and pulse until finely chopped. Transfer to a bowl and stir in vinaigrette and salt. Set aside.

3. Set up grill for direct cooking over high heat (see page 15). Oil grate when ready to start cooking. Arrange the beef slices diagonally on hot, oiled grill. Cook for 2 to 3 minutes per side for medium-rare. (Add 1 minute to each side for medium.) Serve hot with Chimichurri.

INDOOR METHOD:
Prepare meat and Chimichurri as directed. Preheat broiler. Place steak slices on a foil-lined baking sheet or broiler pan. Broil 6 to 8 inches from heat source for 2 to 3 minutes per side for medium-rare. Serve with Chimichurri.

Prime Rib with Blue Cheese-Horseradish Sauce

Prep 10 minutes   **Grill** 2 hours
Stand 10 minutes   **Makes** 6 servings

Prime rib makes a dressy dish for holidays. To feed a crowd, carve the roast from the ribs before cooking and rest it on top of the ribs to grill. The meat slices thinner, and the ribs make extra servings for those who love them. Blue cheese elevates creamed horseradish to a stylish sauce.

1 4½-pound beef rib roast with bones
   Garlic salt, *Lawry's*®
   Ground black pepper, *McCormick*®

FOR BLUE CHEESE-HORSERADISH SAUCE:
1   cup blue cheese salad dressing, *Bob's Big Boy*®
1½   tablespoons prepared horseradish, *Morehouse*®
1½   teaspoons steak sauce, *A.1.*®

INDOOR METHOD:
Preheat the oven to 450 degrees F. Prepare roast as directed. Place roast on roasting rack in a roasting pan. Roast in oven for 30 minutes and then reduce the oven temperature to 325 degrees F. After 1 hour 15 minutes, begin checking temperature (allow 14 to 16 minutes per pound). Meat thermometer inserted in the thickest part of the roast (away from bone) should register 135 degrees F for medium-rare and 150 degrees F for medium. Serve as directed.

1. Set up grill for indirect cooking over medium heat (no direct heat source under roast; see page 15). Season rib roast with garlic salt and pepper to taste. Set aside.

2. Place roast, bone side down, on hot grill over drip pan. Cover grill and cook for 1½ to 2 hours. If using a charcoal grill, add 10 briquettes to each pile of coals after 1 hour. Cover grill and continue cooking for 30 minutes to 1 hour or until meat thermometer inserted in thickest part of the roast (away from bone) registers 135 degrees F for medium-rare or 150 degrees F for medium. Transfer roast to a platter and let stand for 10 minutes before slicing.

3. Meanwhile, for Blue Cheese-Horseradish Sauce, in a medium bowl, stir together blue cheese dressing, horseradish, and steak sauce. Serve with roast.

BBQ Brisket with Guinness® Mop Sauce

Prep 15 minutes   **Grill** 3½ hours
Stand 10 minutes   **Makes** 12 servings

1	6-pound beef brisket
15	whole peeled garlic cloves, *Global Farms®*
2	tablespoons Montreal steak seasoning, *McCormick® Grill Mates®*
2	teaspoons gumbo filé, *Zatarain's®*
1	packet (1.31-ounce) sloppy joe mix, *McCormick®*
2	bottles (12 ounces each) stout, *Guinness®*
1	cup or more apple cider, *TreeTop®*
2	sweet onions, sliced
2	cups barbecue sauce, *KC Masterpiece®*

1. Soak 1 cup hickory or oak wood chips in water for at least 1 hour; drain. Set up grill for indirect cooking over medium heat (no direct heat source under brisket; see page 15).

2. Cut small slits all over brisket and insert garlic cloves. In a small bowl, combine steak seasoning, gumbo filé, and sloppy joe mix. Rub seasoning mixture into brisket and place in foil baking pan. Pour stout over top. Add enough apple cider to cover brisket halfway. Top with onions. Cover with heavy-duty aluminum foil.

3. Place on hot grill over drip pan. Cover grill and cook for 2½ hours. If using charcoal, add 10 briquettes to each pile of coals every hour.

4. Remove brisket and foil pan from grill. Add wood chips to smoke box if using gas grill or place chips onto hot coals if using charcoal. Remove brisket from braising liquid and place directly on grill grate over drip pan. Reserve onions and braising liquid.

5. To make mop sauce, combine 2 cups of the braising liquid with the barbecue sauce. Baste brisket thoroughly with mop sauce. Cover grill. Cook for 1 hour more, turning and basting brisket with sauce every 20 minutes. Transfer brisket to cutting board and let stand for 10 minutes. Thinly slice beef against the grain. Serve with sweet onions and mop sauce on the side.

INDOOR METHOD:
Preheat oven to 375 degrees F. Prepare brisket as directed. Roast in oven for 2½ to 3 hours. Remove brisket from braising liquid and place on foil-lined baking sheet. Reduce oven temperature to 350 degrees F. Combine barbecue sauce with 2 cups braising liquid. Baste brisket with barbecue sauce mixture; return to oven. Roast for 30 minutes more, turning and basting brisket with sauce every 15 minutes. Remove from oven and let stand for 10 minutes. Serve as directed.

Mediterranean Grilled Short Ribs

Prep 15 minutes **Grill** 8 minutes
Stand 30 minutes **Makes** 4 servings

3 tablespoons Greek seasoning, *Spice Islands*®
1 tablespoon garlic powder
1 tablespoon Montreal steak seasoning, *McCormick*® *Grill Mates*®
1 teaspoon onion powder
4 pounds crosscut beef short ribs

FOR BALSAMIC SALSA:
1 can (15-ounce) petite diced tomatoes, drained, *S&W*®
¼ cup olive tapenade, *Cantaré*®
1 tablespoon chopped fresh parsley
2 teaspoons balsamic vinegar

1. In a small bowl, stir together Greek seasoning, garlic powder, steak seasoning, and onion powder. Rub seasoning mixture into short ribs. Cover; chill in refrigerator until ready to grill.

2. Meanwhile, for Balsamic Salsa, in a small bowl, combine tomatoes, tapenade, parsley, and vinegar. Set aside.

3. Set up grill for direct cooking over high heat (see page 15). Oil grate when ready to start cooking. Let ribs stand at room temperature about 30 minutes.

4. Place ribs on hot, oiled grill and cook for 4 to 6 minutes per side for medium. Serve hot with Balsamic Salsa on the side.

INDOOR METHOD:
Prepare short ribs and Balsamic Salsa as directed. Preheat broiler. Place ribs on foil-lined baking sheet or broiler pan. Broil 6 to 8 inches from heat source for 5 to 7 minutes per side for medium. Serve hot with salsa on the side.

South-of-the-Border Smoked Ribs

Prep 25 minutes   **Cook** 5 minutes
Grill 1½ hours   **Makes** 4 servings

1	rack beef back ribs (about 3 pounds)
1	packet taco seasoning mix, *McCormick®*
1	tablespoon Mexican seasoning, *McCormick®*
2	teaspoons granulated garlic
1½	cups All-Purpose Beef BBQ Sauce (see page 107)
1	cup taco sauce (hot or mild), *La Victoria®*

1. Soak 2 cups mesquite wood chips in water for at least 1 hour; drain. Set up grill for indirect cooking over medium heat (no direct heat source under ribs; see page 15).

2. In a small bowl, stir to combine taco seasoning, Mexican seasoning, and garlic. Rub thoroughly into ribs. Set aside.

3. For barbecue sauce, in a medium saucepan, combine All-Purpose Beef BBQ Sauce and taco sauce. Bring to a boil over medium heat. Remove and reserve 1 cup for basting ribs. Set aside.

4. Add some soaked wood chips to smoke box if using gas grill or onto hot coals if using charcoal. Place ribs on rib rack in center of grill over drip pan. Cover and cook for 1½ to 2 hours or until the ribs are tender. If using charcoal, add 10 briquettes to each pile of coals after 1 hour, along with a handful of soaked wood chips. If using a gas grill, add a handful of soaked wood chips to the smoke box every hour.

5. About 30 minutes before ribs are done, remove ribs from rack and place on grill. Baste with the reserved 1 cup barbecue sauce and turn every 10 minutes, basting after each turn. Transfer cooked ribs to platter and cut into serving-size portions. Serve hot with remaining barbecue sauce on the side.

INDOOR METHOD:
Preheat oven to 375 degrees F. Prepare ribs as directed. Place ribs, bone sides up, in a roasting pan; cover with aluminum foil. Roast in oven for 2 hours. Meanwhile prepare BBQ sauce as directed in step 3. If desired, add ¼ teaspoon liquid smoke (*Wright's®*). Remove foil from roasting pan and turn ribs meat sides up. Baste with the reserved 1 cup barbecue sauce and return to oven. Roast for 20 minutes more, turning and basting with sauce every 10 minutes, ending with meat sides up. Serve as directed.

Veal Chops with Cherry BBQ Sauce

Prep 20 minutes
Grill 10 minutes
Makes 4 servings

This is the richest, reddest BBQ sauce you'll find! Bottled sauce is deliciously doctored with cherry preserves and tart pie cherries to make a sweet and tangy syrup that will have tender veal chops zinging with flavor. Sugar burns quickly, so brush on the sauce near the end.

4½	pounds veal loin chops, cut 1 inch thick
1	tablespoon garlic-and-herb seasoning, *Old Bay®*
2	teaspoons salt-free lemon pepper, *McCormick®*

FOR CHERRY BBQ SAUCE:

1	can (15-ounce) red tart pie cherries, drained, *Oregon®*
1	cup barbecue sauce, *Bull's-Eye®*
½	cup cherry preserves, *Smucker's®*

1. Season chops with garlic-and-herb seasoning and lemon pepper. Set aside.

2. For Cherry BBQ Sauce, in a medium saucepan, combine cherries, barbecue sauce, and preserves. Bring to a boil; reduce heat to medium. Simmer for 10 minutes. Remove from heat and cool. Transfer to a food processor and blend until smooth.

3. Set up grill for direct cooking over medium-high heat (see page 15). Oil grate when ready to start cooking. Place chops on hot, oiled grill and cook for 4 to 5 minutes per side. Turn and brush with Cherry BBQ Sauce and cook for 1 minute. Turn and brush with Cherry BBQ Sauce and cook about 1 minute more for medium (160 degrees F).*

4. Remove from heat and brush once more with Cherry BBQ Sauce. Serve hot with Cherry BBQ Sauce on the side.

*TIP: To check for doneness, make a small cut in the thickest part of the meat; it should be slightly less done than you like it. Allow the chops to stand for 5 to 10 minutes (internal temperature will continue to rise slightly), brush with more glaze and serve as directed.

INDOOR METHOD:
Prepare chops and Cherry BBQ Sauce as directed. Place chops on foil-lined baking sheet or broiler pan. Broil 6 to 8 inches from the heat source for 5 to 6 minutes per side. Turn and brush with Cherry BBQ Sauce. Return to broiler and cook for 1 minute. Turn and brush with Cherry BBQ Sauce and cook about 1 minute more for medium (160 degrees F).

Chicken and More

The challenge with chicken—all poultry, really—is keeping it tender and juicy inside and satisfyingly crunchy outside. A spice rub accomplishes both and is healthful too. This chapter has 12 combinations of rubs and marinades that bring together everything you like best about poultry—a delicately charred crust that blends the smoky flavor of the grill with the crisp, peppery breading of old-fashioned pan frying.

My All-Purpose Poultry Sprinkle is a savory blend of garlic, citrus, and herbs that complements all things with wings, from mild, sweet chicken to deeper, darker duck. Try it on top of my Mojo Marinade to rev up chicken, rub it over a tangy margarita brine on turkey, or pair it with a zesty Peri-Peri sauce on game hens. A make-ahead timesaver, it's an effortless way to spritz up a meal and get it on the table at a moment's notice.

The Recipes

All-Purpose Poultry Sprinkle

Prep 5 minutes   **Makes** about ¼ cup

2	tablespoons garlic salt, *Lawry's®*
2	tablespoons citrus-herb seasoning, *Spice Islands®*
2	teaspoons poultry seasoning, *McCormick®*
⅛	teaspoon cayenne pepper, *McCormick®*

1. In an airtight container, combine garlic salt, citrus-herb seasoning, poultry seasoning, and cayenne pepper. Cover and store for up to 4 months.

Greek Stuffed Chicken Breasts

Prep 15 minutes   **Grill** 12 minutes
Stand 30 minutes   **Marinate** 30 minutes
Makes 4 servings

FOR CHEESE STUFFING:

1   container (6-ounce) feta cheese in brine, drained and crumbled, *Athenos*®
2   tablespoons pitted kalamata olives, chopped, *Peloponnese*®
1   tablespoon Greek seasoning, *Spice Islands*®
1   tablespoon capers, drained, *Star*®
    Shredded zest from 1 lemon
2   teaspoons extra-virgin olive oil, *Bertolli*®

FOR CHICKEN:

4   boneless, skinless chicken breast halves
¼   cup extra-virgin olive oil, *Bertolli*®
    Juice from 1 lemon
2   teaspoons lemon pepper, *McCormick*

1. For Cheese Stuffing, in a medium bowl, combine feta cheese, olives, Greek seasoning, capers, lemon zest, and the 2 teaspoons oil. Set aside.

2. Remove tenders from chicken breasts (if attached) and cut a pocket into the side of each breast half, being careful not to cut through. Divide Cheese Stuffing among the 4 breast pockets and secure the pockets with wooden toothpicks.

3. For marinade, in a small bowl, whisk together the ¼ cup oil, lemon juice, and lemon pepper. Place stuffed chicken breasts in a large zip-top bag and pour in marinade. Squeeze air out of bag; seal. Gently massage bag to combine. Marinate in refrigerator for 30 minutes to 2 hours.

4. Set up grill for direct grilling over medium-high heat (see page 15). Oil grate when ready to start cooking. Let chicken stand at room temperature for 30 minutes. Remove chicken from marinade and discard marinade. Place chicken on hot, oiled grill and cook 6 to 8 minutes per side or until chicken is no longer pink and juices run clear (170 degrees F).

INDOOR METHOD:
Prepare chicken as directed. Preheat oven to 375 degrees F. Place chicken on a foil-lined baking sheet. Roast in oven for 25 to 30 minutes or until chicken is no longer pink and juices run clear (170 degrees F).

Chicken Under Bricks

Prep 10 minutes **Grill** 6 minutes
Stand 30 minutes **Marinate** 1 hour
Makes 4 servings

It's called *pollo al mattone*—an old Tuscan technique that presses the chicken flat to the grill, giving it a crisp exterior and a moist, tender interior.

4	boneless, skinless chicken breast halves
1	cup balsamic vinaigrette, *Newman's Own®*
½	cup balsamic vinegar
¼	cup chopped fresh parsley
2	tablespoons frozen orange juice concentrate, thawed, *Minute Maid®*
1	tablespoon Italian seasoning, *McCormick®*
2	teaspoons crushed garlic, *Gourmet Garden®*

1. Wrap 2 bricks in aluminum foil. Rinse chicken under cold water and pat dry with paper towels. Place in a large zip-top bag. Add balsamic vinaigrette, vinegar, parsley, orange juice concentrate, Italian seasoning, and garlic. Squeeze air out of bag and seal. Gently massage bag to combine. Marinate in refrigerator 1 to 4 hours.

2. Set up grill for direct grilling over medium-high heat (see page 15). Oil grate when ready to start cooking. Let chicken stand at room temperature for 30 minutes. Remove chicken from marinade; discard marinade. Place chicken on hot, oiled grill and place foil-wrapped bricks on top (see photo, page 9). Cook 3 to 4 minutes per side or until chicken is no longer pink and juices run clear (170 degrees F).

INDOOR METHOD:
Omit foil-wrapped bricks. Prepare chicken as directed. Preheat broiler. Remove chicken from marinade; discard marinade. Place chicken on foil-lined baking sheet or broiler pan. Broil 6 to 8 inches from heat source for 5 to 6 minutes per side or until chicken is no longer pink and juices run clear (170 degrees F). Do not overcook.

Bourbon-Brined Chicken

Prep 15 minutes **Grill** 10 minutes
Stand 30 minutes **Marinate** 2 hours
Makes 4 servings

1	cup bourbon, *Jim Beam®*
2	tablespoons salt
2	tablespoons packed brown sugar, *C&H®*
2	tablespoons mulling spices, *Spice Hunter®*
1	cup orange juice, *Minute Maid®*
2	teaspoons crushed garlic, *Gourmet Garden®*
4	boneless, skinless chicken breast halves

1. For marinade, in a small saucepan, combine bourbon, salt, brown sugar, and mulling spices. Bring to a boil; reduce heat. Simmer, stirring frequently until salt and sugar are dissolved. Stir in orange juice and garlic. Cool to room temperature.

2. Rinse chicken under cold water and pat dry with paper towels. Place in a large zip-top bag. Pour marinade into bag. Squeeze air out of bag; seal. Gently massage bag to combine. Marinate in refrigerator for 2 to 3 hours.

3. Set up grill for direct grilling over medium-high heat (see page 15). Oil grate when ready to start cooking. Let chicken stand at room temperature for 30 minutes. Remove chicken from marinade; discard marinade. Place chicken on hot, oiled grill and cook for 5 to 6 minutes per side or until chicken is no longer pink and juices run clear (170 degrees F).

INDOOR METHOD:
Prepare as directed. Preheat broiler. Remove chicken from marinade; discard marinade. Place chicken on a foil-lined baking sheet. Broil 6 to 8 inches from heat source for 5 to 6 minutes per side or until chicken is no longer pink and juices run clear (170 degrees F).

Key Lime Grilled Chicken

FOR KEY LIME SAUCE:

½   cup (1 stick) butter
¼   cup key lime juice, *Nellie & Joe's®*
¼   cup chili sauce, *Heinz®*
2   teaspoons All-Purpose Poultry Sprinkle (see page 135)

FOR CHICKEN:

4   pounds meaty chicken pieces
1   tablespoon All-Purpose Poultry Sprinkle (see page 135)

INDOOR METHOD:

Preheat broiler. Prepare chicken and Key Lime Sauce as directed. Place chicken on foil-lined baking sheet or broiler pan. Broil chicken 6 to 8 inches from heat source about 15 to 20 minutes per side or until chicken is no longer pink and juices run clear (180 degrees F), basting with Key Lime Sauce every few minutes until last 2 minutes of cooking. Discard any remaining key lime sauce.

1. Set up grill for direct cooking over medium heat (see page 15). Oil grate when ready to start cooking. For Key Lime Sauce, in a small saucepan melt butter over medium heat. Stir in lime juice, chili sauce, and the 2 teaspoons All-Purpose Poultry Sprinkle. Cook 1 minute. Remove from heat; set aside.

2. Season chicken pieces with the 1 tablespoon All-Purpose Poultry Sprinkle. Place chicken on hot, oiled grill and cook for 18 to 22 minutes per side or until chicken is no longer pink and juices run clear (170 degrees F) for breast halves; 180 degrees F for thighs and drumsticks), basting with Key Lime Sauce every few minutes until last 2 minutes of cooking. Discard any remaining sauce.

Drunken Drumettes

Prep 10 minutes   Grill 12 minutes
Stand 30 minutes   Marinate 3 hours
Makes 4 servings

In Thailand, they're known as *Peek Gai Daeng Mao*—drunken red chicken wings—and natives eat them right off street carts. This honey-nut soy sauce is a sweeter alternative to the spicy-hot bar-and-grill favorite of Buffalo wings.

⅓   cup light rum, *Bacardi®*
⅓   cup honey, *SueBee®*
¼   cup soy sauce, *Kikkoman®*
2   tablespoons Thai chili sauce
1   packet (0.75-ounce) stir-fry seasoning, *Sun Bird®*
2   teaspoons crushed garlic, *Gourmet Garden®*
4   pounds chicken wing drumettes
3   scallions (green onions), finely chopped (optional)
¼   cup chopped peanuts, *Planters®* (optional)

INDOOR METHOD:

Prepare chicken as directed. Preheat broiler. Place chicken on foil-lined baking sheet or broiling pan. Broil 6 to 8 inches from heat source for 12 to 15 minutes or until cooked through, turning occasionally.

1. In a large bowl, combine rum, honey, soy sauce, chili sauce, stir-fry seasoning, and garlic. Add drumettes, tossing to coat. Cover with plastic wrap and marinate in refrigerator for at least 3 hours, preferably overnight.

2. Set up grill for direct cooking over medium-high heat (see page 15). Oil grate when ready to start cooking. Let drumettes stand at room temperature for 30 minutes. Place on hot, oiled grill. Cook for 12 to 18 minutes or until cooked through, turning occasionally. Transfer chicken to a platter. Sprinkle with chopped scallions and peanuts (optional).

Cuban Mojo Chicken Halves

Prep 20 minutes   **Grill** 1 ¼ hours
Stand 30 minutes   **Marinate** 2 hours
Makes 4 servings

FOR MOJO MARINADE:

1   cup lime juice, *ReaLime®*
¾   cup extra-virgin olive oil, *Bertolli®*
¼   cup frozen orange juice concentrate, thawed, *Minute Maid®*
2   tablespoons Jamaican jerk seasoning, *McCormick®*

FOR CHICKEN:

1   4-pound whole roasting chicken
     Garlic salt, *Lawry's®*
     Salt-free lemon pepper, *McCormick®*

FOR ORANGE BASTING SAUCE:

½   cup water
¼   cup frozen orange juice concentrate, thawed, *Minute Maid®*
2   tablespoons lime juice, *ReaLime®*
1   tablespoon crushed garlic, *Gourmet Garden®*
1   tablespoon honey, *SueBee®*
1   fresh habañero chile pepper, finely chopped (see note, page 23)
2   teaspoons Jamaican jerk seasoning, *McCormick®*

1. For Mojo Marinade, in a small bowl, stir together the 1 cup lime juice, oil, ¼ cup orange juice concentrate, and the 2 tablespoons jerk seasoning.

2. Cut chicken in half with kitchen shears, removing backbone (see photo, page 9). Remove excess skin. Rinse under cold water; pat dry with paper towels. Combine chicken and Mojo Marinade in a zip-top bag. Squeeze air out of bag; seal. Gently massage bag to combine. Marinate in refrigerator for 2 to 4 hours.

3. Set up grill for indirect grilling over medium heat (no direct heat source under bird; see page 15). Oil grate when ready to start cooking. Let chicken stand at room temperature for 30 minutes. Remove chicken from marinade and pat dry with paper towels; discard marinade. Season with garlic salt and lemon pepper.

4. For Orange Basting Sauce, in a small bowl, combine the water, the ¼ cup orange juice concentrate, the 2 tablespoons lime juice, garlic, honey, chile pepper, and the 2 teaspoons jerk seasoning. Set aside.

5. Place chicken halves, skin sides up, on hot, oiled grill; cover grill. Cook for 30 minutes. Turn; brush with Orange Basting Sauce. Cook for 45 to 60 minutes more or until chicken is no longer pink and juices run clear (180 degrees F in thigh), turning and brushing with basting sauce every 15 minutes up to the last 15 minutes of grilling. Discard remaining sauce.

INDOOR METHOD:

Preheat oven to 325 degrees F. Prepare chicken and Orange Basting Sauce as directed. Place chicken halves, skin sides up, in roasting pan. Roast chicken in oven about 1½ hours or until chicken is no longer pink and juices run clear (180 degrees F in thigh), brushing with Orange Basting Sauce every 15 minutes up to the last 15 minutes of roasting. Discard any remaining basting sauce.

Tecate® Beer Can Chicken

Prep 15 minutes **Grill** 1¼ hours
Stand 25 minutes **Makes** 4 servings

This creative cooking method is a hit at cookouts. Place an open can of beer in the cavity of a whole chicken and grill it upright. The steam will release the Mexican spice rub and beer-baste the bird from the inside out. Serve with warm tortillas and ice-cold beer with lime for a fiesta feast.

FOR MEXICAN RUB:
2 tablespoons Mexican seasoning, *McCormick®*
1 tablespoon paprika, *McCormick®*
1 tablespoon Montreal chicken seasoning, *McCormick® Grill Mates®*

FOR CHICKEN:
1 4-pound whole roasting chicken
1 can (12-ounce) beer, *Tecate®*
Lime wedges
Warm tortillas

1. Set up grill for indirect cooking (no heat source directly under bird; see page 15) over medium heat.

2. For Mexican Rub, in a small bowl, combine Mexican seasoning, paprika, and chicken seasoning; set aside until ready to use.

3. Remove neck and giblets from chicken cavity. Trim off excess fat. Rinse chicken body cavity under cold water; pat dry with paper towels. Rub chicken generously inside and out with Mexican Rub. Let chicken stand for 15 minutes to allow rub to cure.

4. Open beer; drain one-quarter of the can. Set chicken over the can so that the legs and can form a tripod (see note on vertical roaster, page 13). Carefully place beer can chicken on grill over drip pan. Cover grill and cook 1¼ to 1½ hours or until internal temperature of thigh meat reaches 180 degrees F.

5. Remove from grill and let stand upright for 10 minutes. Carefully slip beer can out of chicken and carve chicken. Serve hot with lime wedges and tortillas.

INDOOR METHOD:
Preheat oven to 325 degrees F. Prepare chicken as directed. Place chicken on beer can on a baking sheet. Roast in oven about 1¾ hours or until internal temperature of thigh meat reaches 180 degrees F. Remove from oven. Tent with foil and let stand for 10 minutes. Carefully remove chicken from beer can and carve.

Lemon-Herb
Grill-Roasted Chicken

Prep 30 minutes
Grill 1 ¼ hours
Stand 10 minutes
Makes 4 servings

FOR LEMON-HERB BUTTER:

6	tablespoons butter, softened
1	tablespoon All-Purpose Poultry Sprinkle (page 135)
1	tablespoon lemon juice, *Minute Maid*®
1	teaspoon crushed garlic, *Gourmet Garden*®
¼	teaspoon lemon zest

FOR CHICKEN:

1	4-pound whole roasting chicken
1	tablespoon salt
1	tablespoon ground black pepper, *McCormick*®
1	packet (0.75-ounce) fresh herbs poultry herb blend (sage, thyme, and rosemary), *Ready Pac*®
1	lemon, thickly sliced

1. For Lemon-Herb Butter, in a small bowl, using a fork, combine softened butter, All-Purpose Poultry Sprinkle, lemon juice, garlic, and lemon zest. Cover and chill in the refrigerator for 15 to 30 minutes or until firm but not hard.

2. Set up grill for indirect cooking over medium heat (no direct heat source under bird; see page 15). Oil grate when ready to start cooking.

3. Remove neck and giblets from chicken cavity. Trim excess fat. Rinse the chicken body cavity under cold water; pat dry with paper towels. Use your finger to carefully loosen the skin around the entire bird.

4. Chop Lemon-Herb Butter into small pieces. Place some of the butter pieces under the skin of the chicken. Rub the remaining butter pieces on the outside of the skin and season with salt and pepper. Stuff the cavity with fresh herbs and lemon slices.

5. Place chicken, breast side up, on hot, oiled grill over a drip pan. Cover grill. Roast for 1 ¼ to 1 ½ hours or until golden brown and internal temperature of thigh meat reaches 180 degrees F. Remove chicken from grill and let stand for 10 minutes before carving.

INDOOR METHOD:
Preheat oven to 350 degrees F. Prepare chicken as directed. Place chicken in roasting pan. Roast in oven about 1½ hours or until golden brown and the internal temperature of thigh meat reaches 180 degrees F. Remove from oven; tent with aluminum foil and let stand for 10 minutes.

Cranberry Turkey Chops

Prep 20 minutes
Grill 8 minutes
Makes 4 servings

1   bone-in turkey breast half, skin removed
1   tablespoon Montreal chicken seasoning, *McCormick® Grill Mates®*
1   tablespoon five-spice powder, *McCormick®*

FOR CRANBERRY SALSA:
1   can (15-ounce) whole cranberry sauce, *Ocean Spray®*
¼   cup chopped fresh cilantro
2   scallions (green onions), finely chopped
2   tablespoons canned chopped jalapeño chile peppers, *Ortega®*
2   tablespoons lime juice, *ReaLime®*

INDOOR METHOD:
Prepare chops and Cranberry Salsa as directed. Preheat broiler. Place chops on a foil-lined baking sheet or broiler pan. Broil 6 to 8 inches from heat source for 4 to 5 minutes per side or until turkey is no longer pink and juices run clear (170 degrees F). Serve as directed.

1. Set up grill for direct cooking over medium-high heat (see page 15). Oil grate when ready to start cooking. Leaving rib bones attached, cut across the turkey breast to make 1-inch-thick chops. Combine chicken seasoning and five-spice powder. Season chops with seasoning mixture. For Cranberry Salsa, in a bowl, break up cranberry sauce with a fork. Stir in cilantro, scallions, chile peppers, lime juice, and ¼ teaspoon *salt*. Season to taste with *ground black pepper*. Set aside until ready to serve.

2. Place chops on hot, oiled grill. Cook for 4 to 5 minutes per side or until turkey is no longer pink and juices run clear (170 degrees F). Serve hot or at room temperature with Cranberry Salsa.

Margarita Turkey

Prep 15 minutes   **Grill** 1 hour
Stand 40 minutes   **Marinate** 4 hours
Makes 4 servings

1   cup water
3   tablespoons salt
3   tablespoons sugar
2   cups ready-to-drink margarita mix, *Jose Cuervo®*
¼   cup chopped fresh cilantro
2   teaspoons crushed garlic, *Gourmet Garden®*
1   2-pound boneless, skinless turkey breast half
     Cilantro sprigs (optional)

INDOOR METHOD:
Preheat oven to 350 degrees F. Prepare turkey breast as directed. Place on foil-lined baking sheet. Roast in oven for 50 to 60 minutes or until internal temperature reaches 170 degrees F. Let stand for 10 minutes before carving.

1. For marinade, in a saucepan, combine the water, salt, and sugar. Bring to a boil; reduce heat. Simmer, stirring frequently, until sugar is dissolved. Stir in margarita mix, the ¼ cup cilantro, and the garlic; cool. Place turkey in a large zip-top bag. Pour marinade over turkey. Seal bag; gently massage. Marinate in refrigerator for 4 to 6 hours.

2. Set up grill for indirect grilling over medium heat (no direct heat source under turkey; see page 15). Oil grate when ready to start cooking. Let turkey stand at room temperature for 30 minutes. Remove turkey from marinade and discard marinade. Place turkey on hot, oiled grill and cover grill. Cook for 1 to 1½ hours or until internal temperature reaches 170 degrees F. Remove from grill and let stand for 10 minutes. Cut into ¼-inch-thick slices. Garnish with cilantro sprigs (optional).

Peri-Peri Spatchcooked Game Hens

Prep 25 minutes Grill 20 minutes
Stand 40 minutes Marinate 2 hours
Makes 4 servings

4	1- to 1½-pound Cornish game hens

FOR PERI-PERI MARINADE:

2	tablespoons fresh oregano leaves
1	tablespoon canned chopped jalapeño chile peppers, *Ortega*®
1	tablespoon crushed garlic, *Gourmet Garden*®
2	teaspoons chopped ginger, *Gourmet Garden*®
1	cup lemon juice, *Minute Maid*®
¼	cup paprika, *McCormick*®
2	teaspoons spicy Montreal steak seasoning, *McCormick*® *Grill Mates*®
¼	cup extra-virgin olive oil, *Bertolli*®

1. Remove the backbone from the game hens with kitchen shears. Open each of the hens and, from the inside, run a knife along each side of the breast bone. Run your finger along the breast bone, pull out, and remove. Cut off wing tips and discard. Rinse hens under cold water and pat dry with paper towels; set aside.

2. For Peri-Peri Marinade, in blender, combine oregano, chile peppers, garlic, and ginger. With the motor running, add enough lemon juice to blend into a paste. Add remaining lemon juice, paprika, and steak seasoning; pulse to combine. With motor running, slowly pour in oil. Reserve ½ cup of marinade for basting. Place hens in a shallow baking dish and rub thoroughly with remaining marinade. Cover and marinate in refrigerator for 2 to 3 hours.

3. Set up grill for direct grilling over medium heat (see page 15). Oil grate when ready to start cooking. Let hens stand at room temperature for 30 minutes. Remove hens from marinade; discard marinade.

4. Place hens, skin sides down, on hot, oiled grill. Cook for 10 minutes; turn hens. Baste liberally with reserved marinade. Discard any remaining marinade. Cook for 10 to 14 minutes more or until internal temperature of thigh meat reaches 180 degrees F. Remove from grill and let stand for 10 minutes.

NOTE: Spatchcooked means to split open (lay flat) for grilling. Peri-Peri literally refers to the African bird's-eye chile and it is used to refer to chile-based sauces and marinades.

INDOOR METHOD:
Prepare game hens as directed. Preheat broiler. Remove game hens from marinade; discard marinade. Place chicken on a foil-lined baking sheet or broiler pan. Broil 6 to 8 inches from heat source for 10 to 12 minutes per side or until internal temperature of thigh meat reaches 180 degrees F.

Planked Duck Breast with Grilled Pineapple Salsa

Prep 25 minutes   **Grill** 20 minutes
Stand 5 minutes   **Makes** 4 servings

4	½-pound duck breasts
½	cup plum sauce, *Dynasty*®
	Salt
	Ground black pepper, *McCormick*®

FOR PINEAPPLE SALSA:

1	can (14-ounce) sliced pineapple in juice, drained, *Dole*®
	Nonstick vegetable cooking spray, *Pam*®
1	teaspoon minced ginger, *Gourmet Garden*®
¼	cup roasted red bell pepper, chopped, *Delallo*®
2	tablespoons finely chopped fresh cilantro
2	scallions (green onions), finely chopped
1	tablespoon rice vinegar, *Marukan*®
¼	teaspoon salt

1. Soak a cedar grilling plank in water for at least 1 hour. Set up grill for direct cooking over medium-high heat (see page 15). Oil grate when ready to start cooking.

2. Pull skin away from each duck breast, leaving it hinged on one side. Brush duck liberally with plum sauce on all sides. Discard any remaining plum sauce. Season with salt and pepper. Lay skin back over and set aside.

3. For Pineapple Salsa, pat drained pineapple dry with paper towels. Spray both sides of slices with cooking spray. Place on hot, oiled grill. Cook for 1 to 2 minutes per side until marked. Remove and let cool. Roughly chop pineapple and place in a medium bowl. Add ginger, bell pepper, cilantro, scallions, vinegar, and salt. Toss to combine; chill in refrigerator until ready to serve.

4. Season the plank by removing plank from the water and placing on hot grill. Cover grill for 3 minutes. Plank may be warped; turn plank every minute until it flattens out.

5. Place duck breasts on the plank, skin sides up. Close grill and cook for 20 to 25 minutes or until internal temperature reaches 155 degrees F. Remove from grill. Let stand for 5 minutes and remove skin. Slice and serve with Pineapple Salsa.

INDOOR METHOD:
Prepare duck as directed, only completely remove the skin. For smoky flavor, add 1 to 2 drops liquid smoke, (*Wright's*®) to the plum sauce. Prepare Pineapple Salsa as directed, omitting grilling the pineapple. Heat a large skillet with 1 tablespoon canola oil (*Wesson*®). Pan sear duck breasts for 2 to 3 minutes per side or until internal temperature reaches 155 degrees F. Let stand 5 minutes before slicing. Serve as directed.

Swimmers

When your objectives are light, healthy, simple, and sophisticated, fish is the dish. There's a fish for everyone, and you can always find new ways to fix it. You can always find new salsas to top it with too. They're a creative, colorful way to give any seafood a boost, enhancing the flavor and the presentation at the same time.

This chapter is a tribute to salsas made simple. Chunky Mango-Avocado Salsa mixes fresh and canned fruits to make grilled snapper bright and beachy. Key Lime Salsa tosses bottled dressing with lime juice and jalapeños to give swordfish a Southwest kick. The sassiest salsas are a fusion of flavors and textures, so boldly mix sweet, tart, hot, and cool to make your taste buds dance.

The Recipes

How to 'Bump-Up' Salsa

You can make ordinary salsa extraordinary by adding canned fruit, fruit juice, and fresh chopped herbs or scallions to bottled salsa. "Heat up" any grilled dish with one of the salsas from the following recipes:

* Jalapeño-Lime Swordfish with Key Lime Salsa
* Grilled Halibut with Pineapple-Tomatillo Salsa
* Grilled Snapper with Mango-Avocado Salsa

Salmon Steaks with Sun-Dried and Fresh Tomato Salsa

Prep 15 minutes
Grill 6 minutes
Makes 4 servings

4 ½ teaspoons packed brown sugar, *C&H®*
1 tablespoon paprika, *McCormick®*
1 tablespoon Montreal chicken seasoning, *McCormick® Grill Mates®*
1 tablespoon Italian seasoning, *McCormick®*
4 6-ounce salmon steaks

FOR SUN-DRIED AND FRESH TOMATO SALSA:
1 cup red cherry tomatoes, cut in half
1 cup yellow pear tomatoes, cut in half
2 tablespoons drained and chopped oil-packed sun-dried tomatoes, *Sonoma®*
2 tablespoons balsamic vinaigrette, *Newman's Own®*
1 tablespoon chopped fresh parsley
Salt
Ground black pepper, *McCormick®*
Nonstick vegetable cooking spray, *Pam®*

1. Set up grill for direct cooking over medium-high heat (see page 15). Oil grate when ready to cook. In a small bowl, combine brown sugar, paprika, chicken seasoning, and Italian seasoning. Rub into all sides of fish steaks. Set aside.

2. For Sun-Dried and Fresh Tomato Salsa, in a large bowl, combine cherry tomatoes, pear tomatoes, sun-dried tomatoes, vinaigrette, and parsley. Season to taste with salt and pepper. Set aside.

3. Spray fish lightly with cooking spray. Place fish on hot, oiled grill. Cook for 3 to 5 minutes per side or until fish flakes easily when tested with a fork. Serve hot with Sun-Dried and Fresh Tomato Salsa.

INDOOR METHOD:
Prepare fish and Sun-Dried and Fresh Tomato Salsa as directed. Preheat broiler. Place fish on a foil-lined baking sheet or broiler pan. Broil 6 to 8 inches from heat source for 3 to 5 minutes per side or until fish flakes easily when tested with a fork. Serve as directed.

Salmon with Lime Butter

Prep 15 minutes
Grill 6 minutes
Makes 4 servings

1   tablespoon seafood seasoning, *Old Bay®*
1   tablespoon salt-free citrus-herb seasoning, *Spice Islands®*
4   6-ounce salmon fillets

FOR LIME BUTTER:
1   lime
6   tablespoons butter, softened
2   teaspoons finely chopped crystallized ginger, *Reed's®*

INDOOR METHOD:
Prepare fish and Lime Butter as directed. Preheat broiler. Place fish on a foil-lined baking sheet or broiler pan. Broil 6 to 8 inches from heat source for 3 to 5 minutes per side or until fish flakes easily when tested with a fork. Serve as directed.

1. Set up grill for direct cooking over medium-high heat (see page 15). Oil grate when ready to cook. In a small bowl, stir together seafood seasoning and citrus-herb seasoning. Season all sides of fish fillets. Set aside. For Lime Butter, using a fine grater, remove zest from lime; set aside. Cut lime in half, squeeze juice from one half. (Reserve remaining lime half for another use.) In a small bowl, use a fork to combine butter, lime zest, lime juice, and ginger. Cover; chill until ready to use. Spray fish lightly with *cooking spray*. Place fish, skin sides down, on hot, oiled grill. Cook for 3 to 5 minutes per side or until fish flakes easily when tested with a fork. Serve hot with Lime Butter.

Spicy Hoisin Tuna Steaks

Prep 20 minutes
Grill 8 minutes
Makes 4 servings

FOR SPICY HOISIN SAUCE:
½   cup hoisin sauce, *Lee Kum Kee®*
2   tablespoons rice vinegar, *Marukan®*
1   tablespoon soy sauce, *Kikkoman®*
2   teaspoons chile blend, *Gourmet Garden®*
1   teaspoon crushed garlic, *Gourmet Garden®*
1   teaspoon minced ginger, *Gourmet Garden®*

FOR TUNA STEAKS:
4   6-ounce tuna steaks
4   teaspoons sesame seeds

INDOOR METHOD:
Prepare Spicy Hoisin Sauce and fish as directed. Preheat broiler. Place fish on foil-lined baking sheet or broiler pan. Broil 6 to 8 inches from heat source about 3 minutes per side or until fish flakes easily when tested with a fork. Serve as directed.

1. Soak a cedar grilling plank in water for at least 1 hour. Set up grill for direct cooking over medium-high heat (see page 15). For Spicy Hoisin Sauce, in a saucepan, combine the ½ cup hoisin sauce, the vinegar, soy sauce, chile blend, garlic, and ginger. Bring to a boil; reduce heat. Simmer for 5 minutes.

2. Season cedar plank by removing plank from the water and placing on hot grill. Cover grill for 3 minutes. Plank may be warped; turn plank every minute until it flattens out. Measure out ⅓ cup of Spicy Hoisin Sauce; brush over fish. Sprinkle with sesame seeds. Place on seasoned plank; cover grill. Cook for 8 to 12 minutes or until fish flakes easily when tested with a fork. Serve tuna hot with remaining Spicy Hoisin Sauce.

Grilled Halibut with Pineapple-Tomatillo Salsa

Prep 20 minutes   **Grill** 6 minutes
Stand 15 minutes   **Marinate** 30 minutes
Makes 4 servings

4	6-ounce halibut fillets
1	cup pineapple juice, *Dole*®
½	cup bottled salsa verde, *La Victoria*®
¼	cup finely chopped fresh cilantro
1	tablespoon Mexican seasoning, *McCormick*®
1	tablespoon lime juice, *ReaLime*®
2	teaspoons crushed garlic, *Gourmet Garden*®

FOR PINEAPPLE-TOMATILLO SALSA:

1	cup bottled salsa verde, *La Victoria*®
1	can (8-ounce) crushed pineapple, drained, *Dole*®
¼	cup chopped fresh cilantro
2	scallions (green onions), finely chopped

1. Place halibut in large zip-top bag. In a medium bowl, combine pineapple juice, the ½ cup salsa verde, ¼ cup cilantro, the Mexican seasoning, lime juice, and garlic. Pour into bag with fish. Squeeze air out of bag; seal. Gently massage bag to combine ingredients. Marinate in refrigerator for 30 minutes to 2 hours.

2. For Pineapple-Tomatillo Salsa, in a medium bowl, combine the 1 cup salsa verde, the pineapple, ¼ cup cilantro, and scallions. Cover; chill in the refrigerator until ready to use.

3. Set up grill for direct cooking over medium heat (see page 15). Oil grate when ready to start cooking. Remove fish from marinade; discard marinade. Let fish stand at room temperature for 15 minutes.

4. Place fish on hot, oiled grill; cover grill. Cook for 3 to 4 minutes per side or until fish flakes easily when tested with a fork. Serve fish hot with Pineapple-Tomatillo Salsa.

INDOOR METHOD:
Prepare fish and Pineapple-Tomatillo Salsa as directed. Preheat broiler. Place fish on foil-lined baking sheet or broiler pan. Broil 6 to 8 inches from heat source for 3 to 4 minutes per side or until fish flakes easily when tested with a fork. Serve as directed.

Grilled Snapper with Mango-Avocado Salsa

Prep 15 minutes   **Grill** 8 minutes
Marinate 30 minutes   **Makes** 4 servings

4	6-ounce snapper fillets
1	can (11.5-ounce) mango nectar, *Kern's*®
½	cup bottled chunky salsa, *Pace*®
¼	cup finely chopped fresh cilantro
1	fresh jalapeño chile pepper, sliced (see note, page 23)
2	whole peeled garlic cloves, crushed, *Global Farms*®
½	teaspoon salt

FOR MANGO-AVOCADO SALSA:

1½	cups frozen mango chunks, finely diced, *Dole*®
1	avocado, peeled, pitted, and diced
1	cup bottled chunky salsa, *Pace*®
¼	cup chopped fresh cilantro
1	tablespoon lime juice, *ReaLime*®
	Salt
	Ground black pepper, *McCormick*®

1. Place snapper fillets in large zip-top bag and add mango nectar, the ½ cup salsa, ¼ cup cilantro, the chile pepper, garlic, and the ½ teaspoon salt. Squeeze air out of bag; seal. Gently massage bag to combine. Marinate in refrigerator for 30 minutes to 2 hours.

2. For Mango-Avocado Salsa, in a medium bowl, combine mango, avocado, the 1 cup salsa, ¼ cup cilantro, and the lime juice. Season to taste with salt and black pepper. Cover; chill until ready to use.

3. Set up grill for direct cooking over medium heat (see page 15). Oil grate when ready to start cooking. Remove fish from marinade; discard marinade. Place fish on hot, oiled grill. Cook for 4 to 5 minutes per side or until fish flakes easily when tested with a fork. Serve fish hot with Mango-Avocado Salsa.

INDOOR METHOD:
Prepare fish and Mango-Avocado Salsa as directed. Preheat broiler. Place fish on foil-lined baking sheet or broiler pan. Broil 6 to 8 inches from heat source for 4 to 5 minutes per side or until fish flakes easily when tested with a fork. Serve as directed.

Thai Snapper Grilled in Banana Leaves

Prep 25 minutes **Grill** 8 minutes
Marinate 1 hour **Makes** 4 servings

Once you discover banana leaves, you'll want to grill everything in them. They lock in moisture and keep a delicate fish like snapper from burning and falling apart in the fire. The cooked fish carries the subtle scent of banana throughout—a sweet complement to the spicy curry-peanut sauce.

4	6-ounce snapper fillets
1	bottle (11.5-ounce) Thai peanut sauce, *House of Tsang*®
¼	cup finely chopped fresh cilantro
1	tablespoon chile garlic sauce, *Lee Kum Kee*®
1	tablespoon lime juice, *ReaLime*®
1	teaspoon curry powder, *McCormick*®
2	packages (8.8 ounces each) precooked rice, *Uncle Ben's*® *Ready Rice*®
4	10×12-inch pieces banana leaves*
	Slivered scallion (green onion) tops (optional)

1. Place snapper in a large zip-top bag; set aside. For marinade, in a medium bowl, combine peanut sauce, cilantro, chile garlic sauce, lime juice, and curry powder. Set aside ½ cup of the marinade for serving. Pour remaining marinade over fish in bag. Squeeze air out of bag; seal. Gently massage bag to combine. Marinate in refrigerator for 1 to 2 hours.

2. Set up grill for direct cooking over medium heat (see page 15). Oil grate when ready to cook. Remove fish from marinade and discard marinade. Set aside.

3. Toast pieces of banana leaf on hot, oiled grill for 10 to 15 seconds per side to make more pliable. Place contents of a half package of rice in center of each banana leaf and top with a piece of fish. Fold in sides, then fold in top and bottom (see photo, page 9). Secure with wooden toothpicks.

4. Place packets on grill. Cook for 4 to 5 minutes per side or until fish flakes easily when tested with a fork. Serve hot with reserved ½ cup marinade. Sprinkle with scallion tops (optional).

NOTE: Banana leaves are available frozen at most Asian or Latin specialty grocers. If banana leaves are not available, substitute heavy-duty aluminum foil.

INDOOR METHOD:
Preheat oven to 400 degrees F. Prepare fish packets as directed. Roast in oven for 10 to 12 minutes or until fish flakes easily when tested with a fork. Serve as directed.

Jalapeño-Lime Swordfish with Key Lime Salsa

Prep 15 minutes   Grill 8 minutes
Stand 15 minutes   Marinate 30 minutes
Makes 4 servings

4	6-ounce swordfish steaks
1	cup olive oil-and-vinegar salad dressing, *Newman's Own®*
½	cup key lime juice, *Nellie & Joe's®*
2	scallions (green onions), finely chopped
2	tablespoons jalapeño hot pepper sauce, *Tabasco®*
1	fresh jalapeño chile pepper, sliced (see note, page 23)
1	teaspoon crushed garlic, *Gourmet Garden®*

FOR KEY LIME SALSA:

1	cup bottled chunky salsa, *Newman's Own®*
⅓	cup finely chopped fresh cilantro
¼	cup key lime juice, *Nellie & Joe's®*
2	scallions (green onions), thinly sliced
1	tablespoon jalapeño hot pepper sauce, *Tabasco®*
	Salt
	Ground black pepper, *McCormick®*

1. Place fish in large zip-top bag. For marinade, in a medium bowl, combine salad dressing, the ½ cup lime juice, the 2 scallions, the 2 tablespoons pepper sauce, chile pepper, and garlic. Pour marinade over fish. Squeeze air out of bag; seal. Gently massage bag to combine. Marinate in refrigerator for 30 minutes to 2 hours.

2. For Key Lime Salsa, in a medium bowl, combine salsa, cilantro, the ¼ cup lime juice, the 2 scallions, and the 1 tablespoon pepper sauce. Season to taste with salt and black pepper. Cover; chill until ready to use.

3. Set up grill for direct cooking over medium heat (see page 15). Oil grate when ready to start cooking. Remove fish from marinade; discard marinade. Let fish stand at room temperature for 15 minutes.

4. Place fish on hot, oiled grill. Cook for 4 to 5 minutes per side or until fish flakes easily when tested with a fork. Serve fish hot with Key Lime Salsa.

INDOOR METHOD:
Prepare fish and Key Lime Salsa as directed. Preheat broiler. Place fish on foil-lined baking sheet or broiler pan. Broil 6 to 8 inches from heat source for 4 to 5 minutes per side or until fish flakes easily when tested with a fork. Serve as directed.

Creole Catfish with Roasted Tomato-Chile Sauce

Prep 25 minutes **Grill** 8 minutes
Marinate 30 minutes **Makes** 4 servings

1 ¼ **pounds catfish fillets**
1 **tablespoon lemon juice, *Minute Maid*®**
1 **teaspoon hot pepper sauce, *Tabasco*®**
2 **tablespoons paprika, *McCormick*®**
1 **tablespoon Cajun seasoning, *McCormick*®**
1 **tablespoon blackened fish seasoning, *Old Bay*®**

FOR ROASTED TOMATO-CHILE SAUCE:
1 **can (15-ounce) roasted diced tomatoes, *Muir Glen*®**
1 **can (7-ounce) roasted diced green chile peppers, *Ortega*®**
½ **cup frozen chopped onions, thawed, *C&W*®**
1 **tablespoon lemon juice, *Minute Maid*®**
2 **teaspoons Cajun seasoning, *McCormick*®**
1 **teaspoon hot pepper sauce, *Tabasco*®**
1 **teaspoon crushed garlic, *Gourmet Garden*®**

1. Set up grill for direct cooking over medium heat (see page 15). Oil grate when ready to start cooking.

2. Sprinkle catfish with 1 tablespoon lemon juice and 1 teaspoon hot pepper sauce; set aside. In a medium bowl, stir together paprika, the 1 tablespoon Cajun seasoning, and the blackened fish seasoning. Coat fish completely with spice mixture. Cover and marinate in refrigerator for 30 minutes.

3. For Roasted Tomato-Chile Sauce, in blender, combine tomatoes, green chile peppers, onions, 1 tablespoon lemon juice, the 2 teaspoons Cajun seasoning, 1 teaspoon hot pepper sauce, and garlic. Cover blender and puree until smooth. Transfer to small saucepan. Bring to a boil; reduce heat. Simmer over medium heat for 10 minutes.

4. Place fish on hot, oiled grill. Cook for 4 to 6 minutes per side or until fish flakes easily when tested with a fork. Remove fish from grill. Serve warm with Roasted Tomato-Chile Sauce.

INDOOR METHOD:
Prepare fish and Roasted Tomato-Chile Sauce as directed. Preheat broiler. Place fish on foil-lined baking sheet or broiler pan. Broil 6 to 8 inches from heat source for 4 to 6 minutes per side or until fish flakes easily when tested with a fork. Serve as directed.

Lobster with Citrus Butter

Prep 15 minutes
Grill 8 minutes
Makes 4 servings

4   lobster tails

FOR CITRUS BUTTER:
1   cup (2 sticks) unsalted butter
2   tablespoons lemon juice, *Minute Maid®*
1   tablespoon lime juice, *ReaLime®*
2   teaspoons fines herbes, *Spice Islands®*
2   teaspoons frozen orange juice concentrate, thawed, *Minute Maid®*
1   teaspoon sea salt

INDOOR METHOD:
Prepare lobster and Citrus Butter as directed. Preheat broiler. Place tails, meat-sides up, on foil-lined baking sheet or broiler pan. Broil 6 to 8 inches from heat source for 4 to 5 minutes. Brush with some of the ⅓ cup Citrus Butter and turn. Broil for 6 to 8 minutes more or until lobster is opaque and cooked through. Do not overcook. Brush with remaining portion of the ⅓ cup Citrus Butter. Serve as directed.

1. Set up grill for direct cooking over medium heat (see page 15). Oil grate when ready to start cooking. Using kitchen shears, split lobster tails in half lengthwise. In a saucepan, melt butter over medium-low heat. Skim foam. Stir in lemon juice, lime juice, fines herbes, orange juice concentrate, and salt. Measure ⅓ cup for basting; set aside remaining butter mixture.

2. Brush meat of lobster tails with some of the ⅓ cup Citrus Butter. Place lobster tails, meat sides down, on hot, oiled grill. Cook for 2 to 3 minutes. Turn shell sides down. Brush with the remaining portion of the ⅓ cup Citrus Butter. Cook for 6 to 7 minutes more or until lobster is opaque and cooked through. Do not overcook. Serve hot with remaining Citrus Butter.

Trout Provençal

Prep 15 minutes   **Grill** 12 minutes
Stand 20 minutes   **Marinate** 30 minutes
Makes 4 servings

4   whole trout (1 pound each), cleaned, with heads and tails removed
      Garlic salt, *Lawry's®*
      Ground black pepper, *McCormick®*
3   lemons, cut into slices and/or wedges
8   rosemary sprigs

FOR GARLIC MARINADE:
1   cup olive oil-and-vinegar salad dressing, *Newman's Own®*
3   tablespoons lemon juice, *Minute Maid®*
1   tablespoon herbes de Provence, *McCormick®*
1   teaspoon crushed garlic, *Gourmet Garden®*

INDOOR METHOD:
Prepare fish as directed. Preheat oven to 450 degrees F. Place fish on foil-lined baking sheet. Roast fish in oven about 30 minutes or until fish flakes easily when tested with a fork. Serve as directed.

1. Lay each fish open; season with garlic salt and pepper to taste. Lay lemon slices inside each fish. Place two sprigs of rosemary in each; close fish with wooden toothpicks. Place fish in a large zip-top bag; set aside. For Garlic Marinade, combine salad dressing, lemon juice, herbes de Provence, and garlic. Pour marinade over fish. Squeeze air out of bag; seal. Gently massage bag. Marinate in refrigerator for 30 minutes to 1 hour. Set up grill for direct cooking over medium heat (see page 15). Oil grate when ready to start cooking. Remove fish from marinade; discard marinade. Let fish stand at room temperature for 20 minutes. Place fish on hot, oiled grill. Cook for 6 to 8 minutes per side or until fish flakes easily when tested with a fork. Serve hot with remaining lemon.

Shrimp with Green Goddess Dipping Sauce

Prep 15 minutes **Grill** 4 minutes
Chill 2 hours **Marinate** 30 minutes
Makes 4 servings

This creamy herbal dressing is a San Francisco treat, a culinary nod to the play *The Green Goddess*. It enjoys a revival here as a something-different dip for shrimp. Parsley, chives, and tarragon tint sour cream-mayonnaise its signature color, with anchovies adding the oomph.

2 **pounds large shrimp, with shells and legs**
½ **cup canola oil, *Wesson*®**
⅓ **cup lemon juice, *Minute Maid*®**
¼ **cup roughly chopped fresh tarragon**
2 **teaspoons crushed garlic, *Gourmet Garden*®**

FOR GREEN GODDESS DIPPING SAUCE:
1 **cup mayonnaise, *Hellmann's*® or *Best Foods*®**
1 **cup sour cream, *Knudsen*®**
¼ **cup finely chopped fresh parsley**
¼ **cup finely chopped fresh chives**
¼ **cup finely chopped fresh tarragon**
2 **tablespoons lemon juice, *Minute Maid*®**
1 **packet (1-ounce) ranch salad dressing mix, *Hidden Valley*®**
   Ice

1. Rinse shrimp under cold water and pat dry with paper towels. In large zip-top bag, combine shrimp, oil, the ⅓ cup lemon juice, ¼ cup tarragon, and the garlic. Squeeze air out of bag; seal bag. Gently massage bag to combine. Marinate in refrigerator for 30 minutes.

2. For Green Goddess Dipping Sauce, in a medium bowl, combine mayonnaise, sour cream, parsley, chives, ¼ cup tarragon, the 2 tablespoons lemon juice, and salad dressing mix. Cover with plastic wrap. Chill in refrigerator until ready to use.

3. Set up grill for direct cooking over medium-high heat (see page 15). Oil grate when ready to start cooking. Remove shrimp from marinade; discard marinade. Place shrimp on hot, oiled grill. Cook for 2 to 3 minutes per side or until shrimp are opaque and cooked through. Do not overcook. To stop cooking, transfer shrimp to large bowl filled with ice. Drain and place shrimp in refrigerator about 2 hours or until completely chilled.

4. Serve cold shrimp on a platter on a bed of ice with Green Goddess Dipping Sauce.*

*****TIP:** Don't forget a bowl for the shrimp shells.

INDOOR METHOD:
Prepare shrimp and Green Goddess Dipping Sauce as directed. Preheat broiler. Remove shrimp from marinade and discard marinade. Place shrimp on foil-lined baking sheet or broiler pan. Broil 4 to 6 inches from heat source for 4 minutes. Turn and broil for 2 to 4 minutes more or until shrimp are opaque and cooked through. Do not overcook. Serve as directed.

Margarita
Shrimp Tostadas

Prep 15 minutes **Grill** 4 minutes
Marinate 30 minutes **Makes** 4 servings

1 pound medium shrimp, peeled and deveined
1 cup ready-to-drink margarita mix, *Jose Cuervo*®
1 lime, sliced
¼ cup finely chopped fresh cilantro
2 teaspoons Mexican seasoning, *McCormick*®

FOR SOUR CREAM SAUCE:
¼ cup sour cream, *Knudsen*®
¼ cup bottled chunky salsa, *Pace*®

FOR TOSTADAS:
1 can (15-ounce) refried black beans, heated in microwave, *Rosarita*®
4 tostada shells, *Mission*®
1 bag (8-ounce) coleslaw mix, *Ready Pac*®
2 tomatoes, diced
Chopped fresh cilantro (optional)

INDOOR METHOD:
Prepare shrimp and Sour Cream Sauce as directed. In a large skillet, heat 2 tablespoons extra-virgin olive oil (*Bertolli*®) over medium-high heat. Remove shrimp from marinade and pat dry with paper towels. Discard marinade. Cook shrimp for 4 to 5 minutes or until opaque and cooked through. Do not overcook. Prepare tostadas as directed.

1. Rinse shrimp under cold water and pat dry with paper towels. Place in large zip-top bag. For marinade, in a medium bowl, combine ready-to-drink margarita mix, lime, the ¼ cup cilantro, and the Mexican seasoning. Pour over shrimp in bag. Squeeze air out of bag; seal. Gently massage bag to combine. Marinate in refrigerator for 30 minutes to 2 hours.

2. For Sour Cream Sauce, in small bowl, combine sour cream and salsa. Cover; chill in refrigerator until ready to serve.

3. Set up grill for direct cooking over medium heat (see page 15). Oil grate when ready to start cooking. Remove shrimp from marinade; discard marinade. Place shrimp on hot, oiled grill. Cook for 2 to 3 minutes per side or until shrimp is opaque and cooked through. Do not overcook. Remove from grill and set aside.

4. For Tostadas, spread beans on tostada shells. Top with coleslaw mix and tomatoes. Add shrimp. Sprinkle with cilantro (optional). Serve with Sour Cream Sauce.

Best Burgers

A thick, juicy, hot-off-the-grill burger is a wonderful way to have a gourmet meal without spending a lot. The secret is to use an inventive mix of lavish, restaurant-style toppings that elevate the most inexpensive of meats into a fine dining experience. Anything is ripe for topping, from hamburgers to fish burgers to charred chicken sliders—using your choice of delicious pantry ingredients. Play up the flavors of any burger with hot sauce, wasabi, or chopped spinach, add a toasted bun and a scoop of Grilled Sweet Potato Salad and you have gloriously redefined the Great American Meal.

The Recipes

Think Inside the Bun

Wow party guests at your next barbecue with interesting toppings for plain burgers. Grab items from your pantry such as sliced pineapple, whole green chile peppers, marinated red peppers or mushrooms, diced seasoned tomatoes, and a jar of tapenade. Also check your refrigerator for open containers of herbed cheese spread (*Alouette*®), hummus, or other prepared spreads.

All-Purpose Burger Aïoli

Prep 5 minutes   **Makes** 1½ cups

1	cup mayonnaise, *Hellmann's*® or *Best Foods*®
¼	cup lemon juice, *Minute Maid*®
2	tablespoons minced garlic, *Gourmet Garden*®
1	tablespoon Dijon mustard, *Grey Poupon*®

1. In a large bowl, combine mayonnaise, lemon juice, garlic, and mustard. Transfer to an airtight container. Store in refrigerator for up to 2 weeks. For a thicker sauce, use 3 tablespoons lemon juice.

Brilliant Bacon Burgers

Prep 15 minutes
Grill 9 minutes
Makes 4 servings

1½ pounds ground beef
½ cup bottled chunky salsa, drained, *Pace*®
2 tablespoons finely chopped fresh cilantro
2 tablespoons real bacon crumbles, *Hormel*®
1 tablespoon canned chopped jalapeño chile peppers, *Ortega*®
1 teaspoon Montreal steak seasoning, *McCormick*®
4 slices pepper Jack cheese, *Tillamook*®
4 onion buns, toasted
   Lettuce leaves, sliced tomatoes, and sliced red onion
   Precooked sliced bacon, crisped in microwave, *Oscar Mayer*®
   Purchased guacamole, *Calavo*®

INDOOR METHOD:
Prepare patties as directed. Preheat broiler. Place patties on a wire rack over foil-lined baking sheet or broiler pan. Broil 6 to 8 inches from heat source for 4 to 5 minutes per side for medium (160 degrees F). Place cheese slices on patties; broil for 1 to 2 minutes more or until cheese is melted. Serve as directed.

1. In a large bowl, combine ground beef, salsa, cilantro, bacon crumbles, chile peppers, and steak seasoning. Mix thoroughly. Form into 4 patties* slightly larger than buns. (Cover and chill if not cooking immediately.)

2. Set up grill for direct cooking over high heat (see page 15). Oil grate when ready to start cooking. Place patties on hot, oiled grill. Cook for 4 to 5 minutes per side for medium (160 degrees F). Place cheese slices on burgers. Cook for 1 to 2 minutes more or until cheese is melted. Serve hot on buns with lettuce, tomatoes, red onion, bacon, and guacamole.

*TIP: To prevent sticking, wet your hands before forming patties.

Pizza Burgers

Prep 15 minutes
Grill 8 minutes
Makes 4 servings

Instead of pizza, have a pizza burger, smothered with melted mozzarella and hearty tomato sauce, then dotted with diced pepperoni and mushrooms on a toasted English muffin.

1½ pounds ground beef
⅓ cup diced pepperoni, *Hormel*®
¼ cup pizza sauce plus extra for topping, *Ragu*®
¼ cup mushroom stems and pieces, chopped, *Green Giant*®
2 teaspoons Italian seasoning, *McCormick*®
4 sandwich-size English muffins, toasted, *Thomas*®
   Sliced tomatoes
4 slices mozzarella cheese, *Sargento*®

INDOOR METHOD:
Prepare patties as directed. Preheat broiler. Place patties on a wire rack over a foil-lined baking sheet. Broil 6 to 8 inches from heat source for 4 to 5 minutes per side for medium (160 degrees F). Serve as directed.

1. Combine ground beef, pepperoni, the ¼ cup pizza sauce, the mushrooms, and Italian seasoning. Mix thoroughly. Form into 4 patties (see tip, above) slightly larger than English muffins.

2. Set up grill for direct cooking over high heat (see page 15). Oil grate when ready to start cooking. Place patties on hot, oiled grill. Cook for 4 to 5 minutes per side for medium (160 degrees F). Serve hot on English muffins with tomatoes and additional pizza sauce; add cheese slices. Top with *fresh basil leaves* (optional).

North Carolina Burgers

Prep 20 minutes
Grill 8 minutes
Makes 4 servings

FOR BURGERS:

1½ pounds ground beef
3 tablespoons barbecue sauce, *Jack Daniel's*®
2 tablespoons chili seasoning, *McCormick*®
1 teaspoon Montreal steak seasoning, *McCormick*® *Grill Mates*®

FOR BBQ SLAW:

3 cups coleslaw mix, *Fresh Express*®
2½ tablespoons All-Purpose Burger Aïoli (page 177)
1 tablespoon barbecue sauce, *Jack Daniel's*®
1 teaspoon cider vinegar, *Heinz*®

FOR SERVING:

4 white hamburger buns, toasted
Yellow mustard, *French's*®
1 can (15-ounce) chili without beans, heated in microwave, *Hormel*®

1. For burgers, in a large bowl, combine ground beef, the 3 tablespoons barbecue sauce, the chili seasoning, and steak seasoning. Mix thoroughly. Form into 4 patties (see tip, page 178) slightly larger than buns. (Cover and chill if not cooking immediately.)

2. For BBQ Slaw, in a medium bowl, thoroughly combine coleslaw mix, All-Purpose Burger Aïoli, the 1 tablespoon barbecue sauce, and the vinegar. Cover with plastic wrap and refrigerate until ready to use.

3. Set up grill for direct cooking over high heat (see page 15). Oil grate when ready to start cooking. Place patties on hot, oiled grill. Cook for 4 to 5 minutes per side for medium (160 degrees F). Serve hot on buns with BBQ Slaw, mustard, and chili.

INDOOR METHOD:
Prepare patties and BBQ Slaw as directed. Preheat broiler. Place patties on a wire rack over a foil-lined baking sheet or broiler pan. Broil 6 to 8 inches from heat source for 4 to 5 minutes per side for medium (160 degrees F). Serve as directed.

Three-Meat Burgers with Chipotle-Cinnamon Ketchup

Prep 20 minutes
Grill 9 minutes
Makes 4 servings

FOR CHIPOTLE-CINNAMON KETCHUP:

¾	cup ketchup, *Heinz*®
1½	teaspoons finely chopped chipotle chile peppers in adobo sauce,* *La Victoria*®
¾	teaspoon ground cinnamon, *McCormick*®

FOR BURGERS:

½	pound lean ground beef
½	pound bulk pork sausage
½	pound ground lamb
¼	cup beer, *Corona*®
2	tablespoons chipotle pepper marinade, *McCormick*® *Grill Mates*®
2	teaspoons finely chopped chipotle chile peppers in adobo sauce,* *La Victoria*®
½	teaspoon ground cinnamon, *McCormick*®
4	slices Monterey Jack cheese, *Tillamook*®
4	hamburger buns
	Whole green chile peppers, *Ortega*® (optional)
	Lettuce leaves, sliced avocado, sliced red onion, and sliced tomatoes (optional)

1. For Chipotle-Cinnamon Ketchup, in a small bowl, stir together ketchup, the 1½ teaspoons chopped chipotle chile peppers, and the ¾ teaspoon cinnamon. Cover with plastic wrap; refrigerate until ready to use.

2. For burgers, in a large bowl, combine ground beef, sausage, ground lamb, beer, chipotle pepper marinade, the 2 teaspoons chipotle chile peppers, and the ½ teaspoon cinnamon. Season with *salt* and *ground black pepper*. Mix thoroughly. Form into 4 patties (see tip, page 178) slightly larger than buns. (Cover and chill if not cooking immediately.)

3. Set up grill for direct cooking over high heat (see page 15). Oil grate when ready to start cooking. Place patties on hot, oiled grill. Cook for 4 to 5 minutes per side or until cooked through (160 degrees F). Place cheese slices on patties; grill for 1 to 2 minutes more or until cheese is melted. Serve hot on buns with Chipotle-Cinnamon Ketchup. Serve with green chile peppers (optional) and lettuce, avocado, onion, and tomato (optional).

*NOTE: Chipotle chile peppers are smoked dried jalapeños and are often found packed in adobo sauce, which is a spicy dark red sauce made from tomatoes and herbs. Chipotle peppers in adobo can be found in the Mexican foods section of the grocery store.

INDOOR METHOD:

Prepare Chipotle-Cinnamon Ketchup and patties as directed. Preheat broiler. Place patties on a foil-lined baking sheet or broiler pan. Broil 6 to 8 inches from heat source for 4 to 5 minutes per side or until cooked through (160 degrees F). Place cheese slices on patties. Broil for 1 to 2 minutes more or until cheese is melted. Serve as directed.

Asian Pork Burgers

Prep 15 minutes
Grill 8 minutes
Makes 4 servings

FOR BURGERS:

1½	pounds ground pork
3	scallions (green onions), finely chopped
2	tablespoons stir-fry seasoning mix, *Sun Bird*®
2	tablespoons sesame seeds
1	teaspoon toasted sesame oil

FOR WASABI AÏOLI:

½	cup All-Purpose Burger Aïoli (see page 177)
1½	teaspoons premade wasabi,* *S&B*®

4	sesame hamburger buns, toasted
	Shredded lettuce and sliced onion

1. For burgers, in a large bowl, combine ground pork, scallions, seasoning mix, sesame seeds, and sesame oil. Mix thoroughly. Form into 4 patties (see tip, page 178) slightly larger than buns. For Wasabi Aïoli, in a small bowl, thoroughly combine All-Purpose Burger Aïoli and wasabi. Set up grill for direct cooking over high heat (see page 15). Oil grate when ready to start cooking. Place patties on hot, oiled grill. Cook for 4 to 5 minutes per side for medium (160 degrees F). Serve hot on toasted buns with lettuce, onion, and Wasabi Aïoli.

*TIP: If you can't find premade wasabi, instead mix wasabi powder with a little water. Wasabi powder is available from McCormick® and is sold in the spice section of the supermarket.

INDOOR METHOD:
Prepare patties and Wasabi Aïoli as directed. In a large skillet, heat 1 tablespoon canola oil (*Wesson*®) over medium heat. When oil is hot, add patties and cook for 6 to 8 minutes per side for medium (160 degrees F). Serve as directed.

Taco Meat Loaf

Prep 20 minutes   Grill 45 minutes
Stand 10 minutes   Makes 4 servings

1½	pounds ground beef
½	cup bread crumbs, *Progresso*®
½	cup Mexican cheese crumbles, *Kraft*®
½	cup bottled chunky salsa, *Ortega*®
1	egg
2	tablespoons chopped fresh cilantro
1	teaspoon crushed garlic, *Gourmet Garden*®
1	packet (1.25-ounce) less-sodium taco seasoning mix, *McCormick*®
2	slices thick-cut bacon, *Oscar Mayer*®

1. Prepare grill for indirect cooking over medium-high heat (no direct heat source under meat loaf; see page 15). In a large bowl, combine ground beef, bread crumbs, cheese crumbles, ¼ cup of the salsa, the egg, cilantro, garlic, and taco seasoning. Poke several holes in bottom of an 8×4×2½-inch foil loaf pan. Shape meat mixture to fit loaf pan; place in pan. Spread the remaining ¼ cup salsa over meat loaf; top with bacon.

2. Place on grill over drip pan; cover grill. Cook for 45 minutes to 1 hour or until internal temperature reaches 160 degrees F. Transfer meat loaf to cutting board and let stand for 10 minutes. Remove from loaf pan and slice. Serve warm.

INDOOR METHOD:
Preheat oven to 400 degrees F. Poke holes in bottom of foil loaf pan. Follow directions for mixing, shaping, and placing meat loaf in loaf pan. If desired, add ¼ teaspoon liquid smoke (*Wright's*®) to meat mixture. Place loaf pan on wire rack inside a 13×9×2-inch baking pan and bake for 45 minutes. Serve as directed.

Spicy Italian Sausage Burgers

Prep 30 minutes
Grill 8 minutes
Makes 4 servings

FOR BURGERS:
1¼	pounds Italian sausage, casings removed
1	tablespoon Italian salad dressing mix, *Good Seasons*®
½	to ¾ teaspoon crushed red pepper flakes, *McCormick*®
½	teaspoon garlic powder

FOR EGGPLANT:
1½	cups vegetable oil, *Wesson*®
¼	cup all-purpose flour
2	eggs, beaten
½	cup Italian-seasoned bread crumbs, *Progresso*®
2	Japanese eggplants, cut lengthwise into ⅛-inch-thick slices

½	of a white onion, sliced
4	sandwich rolls, toasted
½	cup All-Purpose Burger Aïoli (see page 177)
1	cup roasted red bell pepper, cut into thin strips, *Delallo*®

1. For burgers, in a large bowl, combine sausage, salad dressing mix, red pepper flakes, and garlic powder. Mix thoroughly. Form into 4 oval patties (see tip, page 178) slightly larger than rolls. (Cover and chill if not cooking immediately.)

2. For eggplant, in a large, deep skillet, heat ¼ inch vegetable oil to 375 degrees F. Place flour, eggs, and bread crumbs in separate shallow bowls. Dredge eggplant slices in flour, shaking off excess. Dip slices into egg, then in bread crumbs. Gently place breaded eggplant in hot oil. Fry until lightly golden on both sides. Remove eggplant slices and let drain on paper towels. Set aside.

3. Set up grill for direct cooking over high heat (see page 15). Oil grate when ready to start cooking. Place patties and onion slices on hot, oiled grill. Cook for 4 to 5 minutes per side or until burgers and onion slices are cooked through (160 degrees F).

4. Place burgers on toasted sandwich roll bottoms. Top each burger with onion slices, eggplant, and All-Purpose Burger Aïoli. Add red bell peppers and roll tops.

INDOOR METHOD:
Prepare patties as directed. Bread and fry eggplant. Preheat broiler. Place patties on a foil-lined baking sheet or broiler pan. Broil 6 to 8 inches from heat source for 4 to 5 minutes per side or until burgers are cooked through (160 degrees F). Serve as directed.

Greek Lamb Burgers with Spinach Aïoli

Prep 15 minutes
Grill 6 minutes
Makes 4 servings

FOR SPINACH AÏOLI:
¼ cup frozen chopped spinach, thawed, *Birds Eye*®
½ cup All-Purpose Burger Aïoli (see page 177)

FOR BURGERS:
1½ pounds ground lamb
¼ cup olive tapenade, *Cantaré*®
1 tablespoon Greek seasoning, *McCormick*®
1 teaspoon crushed garlic, *Gourmet Garden*®
½ teaspoon salt
½ teaspoon ground black pepper, *McCormick*®
4 pita bread rounds, *Sara Lee*®
2 cups mixed baby greens, *Fresh Express*®
Sliced tomatoes and thinly sliced red onion

1. For Spinach Aïoli, prepare spinach according to package directions; drain well. In a medium bowl, mix together spinach and All-Purpose Burger Aïoli. Cover and chill until ready to use.

2. For burgers, in a large bowl, combine ground lamb, tapenade, Greek seasoning, garlic, salt, and pepper. Mix thoroughly. Form into 4 patties (see tip, page 178) of equal size. (Cover and chill if not cooking immediately.)

3. Set up grill for direct cooking over high heat (see page 15). Oil grate when ready to start cooking.

4. Place burgers on hot, oiled grill. Cook for 3 to 4 minutes per side for medium (160 degrees F). Serve hot on pita bread with greens, tomatoes, red onion, and Spinach Aïoli.

INDOOR METHOD:
Prepare Spinach Aïoli and patties as directed. Preheat broiler. Place patties on a wire rack over foil-lined baking sheet or broiler pan. Broil 6 to 8 inches from heat source for 4 to 5 minutes per side for medium (160 degrees F). Serve as directed.

Blackened Chicken Sliders with Cajun Aïoli

Prep 20 minutes
Grill 4 minutes
Makes 4 servings

Forget the drive-thru! A few shakes of hot sauce, Cajun spices, and scallions, a coat of Old Bay® seasoning to blacken, and you're dining down on the bayou. Delete the bun, add grilled onions and peppers, and you have a lean lunch or dinner.

FOR CAJUN AÏOLI:
½   cup All-Purpose Burger Aïoli (see page 177)
1   scallion (green onion), finely chopped
½   teaspoon Cajun seasoning, *McCormick*®
½   teaspoon hot pepper sauce, *Tabasco*®

FOR CHICKEN SLIDERS:
1½   pounds ground chicken
2   scallions (green onions), finely chopped
2   teaspoons Cajun seasoning, *McCormick*®
1   teaspoon hot pepper sauce, *Tabasco*®
½   teaspoon salt
½   teaspoon ground black pepper, *McCormick*®
   Blackened seasoning, *Old Bay*®
   Lettuce leaves, sliced tomatoes, and slivered red onion
12   sourdough dinner rolls, halved horizontally and toasted

1. For Cajun Aïoli, in small bowl, mix together All-Purpose Burger Aïoli, the 1 scallion, the ½ teaspoon Cajun seasoning, and the ½ teaspoon hot pepper sauce. Cover with plastic wrap and refrigerate until ready to use.

2. For Chicken Sliders, in a large bowl, combine ground chicken, the 2 scallions, the 2 teaspoons Cajun seasoning, the 1 teaspoon hot pepper sauce, the salt, and black pepper. Mix thoroughly. Form into 12 miniature patties (see tip, page 178) slightly larger than dinner rolls. (Cover and chill if not cooking immediately.)

3. Place blackened seasoning on a small plate and dip each patty into seasoning, lightly coating each side. Set up grill for direct cooking over medium-high heat (see page 15). Oil grate when ready to start cooking.

4. Place patties on hot, oiled grill. Cook for 2 to 3 minutes per side or until no longer pink inside (165 degrees F). Serve hot on dinner rolls with lettuce, tomatoes, onion, and Cajun Aïoli.

INDOOR METHOD:
Prepare Cajun Aïoli and Chicken Sliders as directed. Preheat broiler. Place patties on a foil-lined baking sheet or broiler pan. Broil 6 to 8 inches from heat source for 3 to 4 minutes per side or until no longer pink inside (165 degrees F). Serve as directed.

Tropical Turkey Burgers with Mango Aïoli

Prep 20 minutes
Grill 10 minutes
Makes 4 servings

FOR BURGERS:

1 ¼	pounds ground turkey breast, *Jennie-O®*
¼	cup finely chopped fresh cilantro
2	tablespoons teriyaki sauce, *Kikkoman®*
2	teaspoons Caribbean jerk seasoning, *McCormick®*

FOR MANGO AÏOLI

¾	cup refrigerated sliced mango, chopped, *Del Monte®*
½	cup All-Purpose Burger Aïoli (see page 177)
1	teaspoon lemon juice, *Minute Maid®*
1	teaspoon Caribbean jerk seasoning, *McCormick®*

4	onion-topped hamburger buns, toasted
	Lettuce leaves
1	can (8-ounce) sliced pineapple in juice, drained, *Dole®*

1. For burgers, in a large bowl, combine ground turkey, cilantro, teriyaki sauce, and the 2 teaspoons jerk seasoning. Mix thoroughly. Form into 4 patties (see tip, page 178) slightly larger than buns. (Cover with plastic wrap and refrigerate if not cooking immediately.)

2. For Mango Aïoli, in a small bowl, combine mango, All-Purpose Burger Aïoli, lemon juice, and the 1 teaspoon jerk seasoning. Cover with plastic wrap and refrigerate until ready to use.

3. Set up grill for direct cooking over medium-high heat (see page 15). Oil grate when ready to start cooking. Place patties on hot, oiled grill. Cook for 5 to 6 minutes per side or until no longer pink inside (165 degrees F). Serve hot on toasted onion buns with lettuce, drained pineapple, and Mango Aïoli.

INDOOR METHOD:
Prepare patties and Mango Aïoli as directed. In a large skillet, heat 1 tablespoon canola oil (*Wesson®*) over medium-high heat. When oil is hot, add patties and cook for 5 to 7 minutes per side or until no longer pink inside (165 degrees F). Serve as directed.

Tinseltown Turkey Burgers

Prep 20 minutes
Grill 10 minutes
Makes 4 servings

FOR BURGERS:

1¼   pounds ground turkey
2   teaspoons lemon juice, *Minute Maid®*
2   teaspoons fines herbes, *Spice Islands®*
1   teaspoon Montreal chicken seasoning, *McCormick® Grill Mates®*
¾   teaspoon salt
½   teaspoon crushed garlic, *Gourmet Garden®*

FOR HERBED AÏOLI:

½   cup All-Purpose Burger Aïoli (see page 177)
2¼   tablespoons Dijon mustard, *Grey Poupon®*
2   teaspoons fines herbes, *Spice Islands®*

FOR SERVING:

4   whole wheat hamburger buns
     Lettuce leaves
     Sliced tomatoes

1. For burgers, in a large bowl, combine ground turkey, lemon juice, 2 teaspoons fines herbes, the chicken seasoning, salt, and garlic. Mix thoroughly. Form into 4 patties (see tip, page 178) slightly larger than buns. (Cover with plastic wrap and refrigerate if not cooking immediately.)

2. For Herbed Aïoli, in a small bowl, stir together All-Purpose Burger Aïoli, mustard, and 2 teaspoons fines herbes. Cover with plastic wrap and refrigerate until ready to use.

3. Set up grill for direct cooking over high heat (see page 15). Oil grate when ready to start cooking.

4. Place patties on hot, oiled grill. Cook for 5 to 6 minutes per side or until no longer pink inside (165 degrees F). Serve hot on buns with lettuce, tomatoes, and Herbed Aïoli.

INDOOR METHOD:
Prepare patties and Herbed Aïoli as directed. In a large skillet, heat 1 tablespoon canola oil (*Wesson®*) over medium-high heat. When oil is hot, add patties and cook for 5 to 7 minutes per side or until no longer pink inside (165 degrees F). Serve as directed.

Fish Burgers with Key Lime Tartar Sauce

Prep 20 minutes
Grill 6 minutes
Makes 4 servings

This healthful burger will make you a fish fan. Old Bay® seasoning gives it the spiciness of a crabfest, while key lime juice injects a contrasting coolness that brings out the inner sweetness of a white fish like halibut. Swap coleslaw and cilantro-spiked tartar sauce for lettuce and mayo.

FOR KEY LIME TARTAR SAUCE:
½   cup tartar sauce, *Hellmann's*® or *Best Foods*®
1   tablespoon bottled key lime juice, *Nellie & Joe's*®
1   tablespoon finely chopped fresh cilantro

FOR BURGERS:
1½   pounds halibut fillets, bones removed
1   egg, lightly beaten
2   tablespoons finely chopped fresh cilantro
4   saltine crackers, crumbled, *Sunshine*®
1   tablespoon bottled key lime juice, *Nellie & Joe's*®
2   teaspoons seafood seasoning, *Old Bay*®
1   teaspoon canola oil, *Wesson*®
   Salt
   Ground black pepper, *McCormick*®
4   white hamburger buns
   Coleslaw mix, *Ready Pac*®
   Fresh cilantro sprigs (optional)

1. For Key Lime Tartar Sauce, in a small bowl, combine tartar sauce, 1 tablespoon lime juice, and the 1 tablespoon cilantro. Cover with plastic wrap. Refrigerate until ready to use.

2. For burgers, cut fish into small pieces, place in food processor and pulse until coarsely minced (do not overprocess).

3. In a large bowl, combine minced fish, egg, the 2 tablespoons cilantro, the crackers, 1 tablespoon lime juice, the seafood seasoning, and oil. Season with salt and pepper. Mix thoroughly. Form mixture into 4 patties (see tip, page 178) slightly larger than buns. (Cover with plastic wrap and refrigerate if not cooking immediately.)

4. Set up grill for direct cooking over medium-high heat (see page 15). Oil grate when ready to cook. Place patties on hot, oiled grill. Cook for 3 to 4 minutes per side or until done. (Be careful not to overcook because burgers will dry out.)

5. Serve hot on buns with coleslaw and Key Lime Tartar Sauce. Top with cilantro sprigs (optional).

INDOOR METHOD:
Prepare Key Lime Tartar Sauce and patties as directed. Preheat broiler. Place patties on a foil-lined baking sheet or broiler pan lightly sprayed with nonstick vegetable cooking spray (*Pam*®). Broil 6 to 8 inches from heat source for 3 to 4 minutes per side or until done. (Be careful not to overcook because burgers will dry out.) Serve as directed.

Desserts and Sweets

If you think the aroma of wood smoke is enticing, wait until you smell these dishes. Dessert on the grill is a treat for all tastes. Peach Melba transitions flawlessly with a wine-soaked plank and a chic Chambord® sauce. Tropical Fruit Kabobs are caramelized then dunked in spicy lime yogurt. Mixed Berry Cobbler is skillet-baked to crumbly perfection … right on the grate.

Then there's chocolate. Thick, glossy and deliciously decadent, my Champion Chocolate Sauce goes with almost any dessert in this chapter, from Grilled Banana Splits to Crepes with Grilled Nectarines. Keep a container on hand to dress up a dish of ice cream after dinner, or drizzle it over a thawed frozen pound cake or cheesecake when you want something a little more special. To really glam it up, swap coffee or fruit liqueur for the vanilla, and be prepared to offer seconds!

The Recipes

Champion Chocolate Sauce

Start to Finish 10 minutes   **Makes** about 1¼ cups

1   cup heavy cream
¾   cup semisweet chocolate chips, *Ghirardelli®*
½   teaspoon vanilla extract, *McCormick®*

1. In a medium saucepan, combine cream and chocolate chips. Cook and stir over medium-low heat until chocolate has melted and is incorporated into cream. Remove from heat and stir in vanilla. Let cool. Transfer to an airtight container. Store in refrigerator for up to 2 weeks. If desired, slowly reheat in microwave oven.

Chocolate Hazelnut Pizza with Strawberries

Prep 10 minutes
Grill 8 minutes
Makes 6 servings

INDOOR METHOD:

Preheat oven to 425 degrees F. Lightly spray baking sheet with nonstick vegetable cooking spray (*Pam®*); set aside. Carefully remove dough from can. Unroll dough and place on baking sheet. Press out dough with fingers to form a 13×9-inch rectangle. Bake in oven for 7 to 10 minutes or until crust begins to brown. Remove crust from oven. Serve as directed.

1	can (13.8-ounce) refrigerated pizza crust dough, *Pillsbury®*
¾	cup chocolate-hazelnut spread, *Nutella®*
1	pound fresh strawberries, cut up
2	tablespoons sliced almonds

1. Set up grill for direct cooking over medium heat (see page 15). Oil grate when ready to start cooking.

2. Carefully remove dough from can. Unroll dough and place on hot, oiled grill. Cook for 3 minutes. Using a cookie sheet as a spatula, turn over crust. Cover and cook for 5 to 7 minutes more or until crust begins to brown.

3. Spread crust with chocolate-hazelnut spread and top with strawberries and almonds. Cut into pieces.

Mixed Berry Cobbler

Prep 20 minutes   **Grill** 20 minutes
Cool 1 hour   **Makes** 8 servings

1½	cups baking mix, *Bisquick®*
1½	cups sugar
¾	cup strawberry nectar, *Kern's®*
1	teaspoon vanilla extract, *McCormick®*
½	cup (1 stick) butter
1	can (21-ounce) strawberry pie filling, *Comstock® More Fruit®*
1	cup frozen mixed berries, thawed, *Dole®*
	Vanilla ice cream (optional)

1. Set up grill for direct cooking over medium heat (see page 15). In a large bowl, combine baking mix, ¾ cup of the sugar, the strawberry nectar, and vanilla extract. Whisk until smooth. Set aside.

2. Place a 10-inch cast-iron skillet on the hot grill and add butter. When butter has melted, stir in remaining ¾ cup sugar. When sugar mixture begins to bubble, stir in pie filling and thawed berries. Pour baking mix batter over top of berries.

3. Close grill and bake for 20 to 30 minutes or until golden brown and toothpick inserted into top crust comes out clean. Remove from grill. Cool for 1 hour. Serve cobbler warm with vanilla ice cream (optional).

INDOOR METHOD:
Preheat oven to 350 degrees F. Prepare baking mix batter as directed; set aside. Follow directions for preparing berry mixture, except use a saucepan and cook over medium-high heat until it begins to bubble. Transfer to a 2-quart baking dish. Pour baking mix batter over top of berry mixture. Place cobbler in oven. Bake for 35 to 40 minutes or until golden brown and a toothpick inserted into the top crust comes out clean. Remove from oven; cool for 1 hour. Serve as directed.

Grilled Pears and Pound Cake

Prep 15 minutes
Grill 2 minutes
Makes 8 servings

1	loaf (16-ounce) frozen pound cake, thawed, *Sara Lee*®
½	cup dark rum, *Myers's*®
	Butter, softened
1	cup caramel ice cream topping, *Hershey's*®
2	cans (29 ounces each) pear halves, drained, *Del Monte*®
	Nonstick vegetable cooking spray, *Pam*®
	Whipped topping, *Cool Whip*®

INDOOR METHOD:

Prepare Rum-Caramel Sauce as directed. Preheat broiler. Line two baking sheets with foil; spray one sheet with nonstick cooking spray. Place the pound cake slices on ungreased baking sheet and pears on the sprayed baking sheet. Broil pound cake 6 to 8 inches from heat for 2 to 3 minutes per side or until toasted. Broil pears 6 to 8 inches from heat source for 1 to 2 minutes per side. Serve as directed.

1. Set up grill for direct cooking over medium heat (see page 15). Oil grate when ready to cook. Using a wooden skewer, poke holes all over top of pound cake. Drizzle ¼ cup of the rum, 1 tablespoon at a time, over pound cake. Trim ends off pound cake; cut pound cake crosswise into 8 slices. Butter both sides of each slice. Place pound cake slices on hot, oiled grill. Cook for 1 to 2 minutes per side or until lightly toasted; set aside.

2. For Rum-Caramel Sauce, in a small skillet or pan, heat remaining ¼ cup rum over medium heat until reduced to 1 tablespoon. In a small bowl, stir reduced rum into caramel topping. Set aside.

3. Cut pear halves in half. Pat dry with paper towels. Lightly spray pear pieces with cooking spray. Place pears on hot, oiled grill. Cook for 1 to 2 minutes per side or until warm and marked on all sides. Toss pears with 2 tablespoons of the Rum-Caramel Sauce. On each of 8 dessert plates, place 1 slice of grilled pound cake and 4 pear pieces. Drizzle with additional sauce and top with whipped topping.

Crepes with Grilled Nectarines

Prep 20 minutes
Grill 6 minutes
Makes 8 servings

Nectarines are smooth-skinned peaches. No need to peel—just pop them right on the grill. Their red-gold colors contrast beautifully with blueberries and look stunning against the white chocolate filling and pools of Butterscotch-Chocolate Sauce. Show this one off when presentation matters.

2	cups low-fat milk
1	box (4-serving-size) fat-free sugar-free instant white chocolate pudding mix, *Jell-O®*
1	teaspoon orange extract, *McCormick®*
4	firm, barely ripe nectarines
	Nonstick vegetable cooking spray, *Pam®*
8	premade crepes, *Frieda®*
1	cup fresh blueberries
1	recipe Butterscotch-Chocolate Sauce (see below)

1. For pudding, in a large bowl, whisk together milk, pudding mix, and orange extract for 2 minutes. Cover with plastic wrap and store in the refrigerator until ready to use. Prepare Butterscotch-Chocolate Sauce.

2. Set up grill for direct cooking over medium heat (see page 15). Oil grate when ready to start cooking. Pit nectarines; cut into eighths. Spray slices lightly with nonstick vegetable cooking spray. Place on hot, oiled grill. Cook for 2 to 3 minutes per side or until warm and soft. Remove from grill; set aside. Place 4 crepes on grill. Cook for 30 seconds per side. Remove from grill; set aside. Repeat with the remaining 4 crepes.

3. Top each crepe with ¼ cup of the pudding and 4 nectarine slices; sprinkle with blueberries. Fold each crepe in quarters. Place a crepe on each of 8 dessert plates. Drizzle each with Butterscotch-Chocolate Sauce.

BUTTERSCOTCH-CHOCOLATE SAUCE: Prepare Champion Chocolate Sauce (see page 199) as directed, except substitute ¼ cup butterscotch chips (*Nestlé®*) for ¼ cup of the chocolate chips.

INDOOR METHOD:
Prepare pudding and Butterscotch-Chocolate Sauce as directed. Heat crepes according to package directions. Preheat broiler. Spray a baking sheet with nonstick cooking spray. Broil pitted, cut nectarines on prepared baking sheet 6 to 8 inches from heat source for 2 to 3 minutes per side. Serve as directed.

Grilled Pineapple Sundae with Chocolate-Rum Sauce

Prep 20 minutes   Grill 4 minutes
Marinate 30 minutes   Makes 4 servings

FOR CHOCOLATE-RUM SAUCE:
1   recipe Champion Chocolate Sauce (see page 199)
¼   cup spiced rum, *Captain Morgan®*

FOR SUNDAE:
1   container (16-ounce) fresh pineapple spears, *Ready Pac®*
¾   cup spiced rum, *Captain Morgan®*
¼   teaspoon pumpkin pie spice, *McCormick®*
    Nonstick vegetable cooking spray, *Pam®*
1   pint vanilla bean ice cream, *Häagen-Dazs®*
¼   cup chopped macadamia nuts, *Mauna Loa®*

1. For Chocolate-Rum Sauce, prepare Champion Chocolate Sauce as directed. Remove from heat. In a small saucepan, heat the ¼ cup rum over medium heat until reduced to 2 tablespoons. Return Champion Chocolate Sauce to medium-low heat and stir in rum until smooth. Set aside.

2. Place pineapple spears in a large zip-top bag. Add the ¾ cup rum and the pie spice. Squeeze air out of bag and seal. Gently massage bag to combine ingredients. Marinate in refrigerator for 30 minutes to overnight.

3. Set up grill for direct cooking over medium heat (see page 15). Oil grate when ready to start cooking.

4. Remove pineapple from marinade and pat dry with paper towels. Spray pineapple lightly with cooking spray. Place pineapple on hot, oiled grill. Cook for 2 to 3 minutes per side or until warm and marked on all sides.

5. Divide grilled pineapple among 4 dessert dishes. Add a scoop of ice cream to each dish and top with Chocolate-Rum Sauce and macadamia nuts.

INDOOR METHOD:
Prepare Chocolate-Rum Sauce and pineapple as directed. Preheat broiler. Place pineapple on a foil-lined baking sheet or broiler pan that has been sprayed with nonstick cooking spray. Broil pineapple 6 to 8 inches from heat source for 2 to 3 minutes per side or until warm. Serve as directed.

Grilled Banana Splits

Prep 20 minutes
Grill 2 minutes
Makes 4 servings

Growing up, a banana split was the answer to all of life's ills. It still is. My version has two secrets—pineapples pan-sautéed in dark rum to give them a crystallized crunch and warm bananas, grilled in the peel, with a pocket of pumpkin pie spice that releases a heavenly aroma.

FOR PINEAPPLE SAUCE:
1	tablespoon butter
1	can (8-ounce) crushed pineapple, *Dole*®
2	tablespoons dark rum, *Meyers's*®
1	recipe Champion Chocolate Sauce (see page 199)
4	unpeeled bananas
½	teaspoon pumpkin pie spice, *McCormick*®
1	quart vanilla ice cream, *Häagen-Dazs*®
1	cup frozen sweetened sliced strawberries, thawed, *Dole*®
	Whipped topping, *Cool Whip*®
¼	cup nut topping, *Diamond*®
12	maraschino cherries

1. For Pineapple Sauce, in a medium skillet over medium-high heat, melt butter. Remove from heat and stir in crushed pineapple and rum. Return to heat and cook until most of the liquid has evaporated and pineapple has begun to caramelize. Remove from heat and cool. Prepare Champion Chocolate Sauce.

2. Cut bananas in half lengthwise, but do not cut through bottom skin. Open up bananas slightly and sprinkle some of the pumpkin pie spice into the center of each. Close bananas.

3. Set up grill for direct cooking over medium heat (see page 15). Oil grate when ready to start cooking.

4. Place bananas on hot, oiled grill. Cook for 2 to 3 minutes or until the skins are dark and bananas are warm, turning once. Remove from grill.

5. Open banana peels and remove bananas. Put 2 halves into each of 4 banana split dishes or oblong bowls. Top each with 3 scoops of ice cream. Spoon Pineapple Sauce and Champion Chocolate Sauce over ice cream. Top with strawberries, whipped cream, nut topping, and cherries.

INDOOR METHOD:
Prepare Pineapple Sauce and bananas as directed. Preheat broiler. On a foil-lined baking sheet, broil bananas 6 to 8 inches from heat source for 2 to 3 minutes, turning once. Serve as directed.

Planked Peaches with Chambord® Melba Sauce

Prep 15 minutes
Grill 7 minutes
Makes 4 servings

1	cup frozen raspberries, thawed, *Dole*®
3	tablespoons sugar
2	tablespoons seedless raspberry jam, *Smucker's*®
2	tablespoons black raspberry liqueur, *Chambord*®
1	can (28-ounce) peach halves, drained, *Del Monte*®
	Vanilla ice cream (optional)

1. Soak a cedar grilling plank in water for at least 1 hour.

2. For Chambord® Melba Sauce, in blender, puree raspberries. Strain through a fine-mesh strainer into a small saucepan. Add 2 tablespoons of the sugar, the jam, and Chambord®. Bring to a boil, reduce heat. Simmer, stirring constantly, until jam has melted and sugar is dissolved. Set aside.

3. Set up grill for direct cooking over medium-high heat (see page 15).

4. Remove plank from water. Place on hot grill. Cover grill for 3 minutes. Plank may be warped. Turn plank every minute until it flattens out.

5. Place peaches, cut sides up, on plank. Sprinkle with the remaining 1 tablespoon sugar. Place on hot grill. Cover grill. Cook for 7 to 8 minutes or until peaches are warm and sugar is just starting to caramelize.

6. Serve immediately with Chambord® Melba Sauce and vanilla ice cream (optional).

INDOOR METHOD:
Preheat broiler. Omit grilling plank. Prepare Chambord® Melba Sauce as directed. Spray a foil-lined baking sheet with nonstick cooking spray. Broil peaches, cut sides down, 6 to 8 inches from heat source for 1 minute. Turn and sprinkle with the 1 tablespoon sugar. Cook another 4 to 5 minutes or until sugar has begun to caramelize. Serve as directed.

Grilled Figs with Orange-Honey Drizzle

Prep 10 minutes
Grill 2 minutes
Makes 4 servings

This effortlessly elegant dish is very "French," where dessert is often a cheese plate. The ripe earthiness of grilled-on-the-grate figs is a heady companion to softened Brie, finished with cascades of orange and honey. Try it for breakfast or anytime you want something naturally sweet.

FOR ORANGE-HONEY DRIZZLE
¼   **cup honey, *SueBee*®**
2   **teaspoons frozen orange juice concentrate, thawed, *Minute Maid*®**
⅛   **teaspoon herbes de Provence, *McCormick*®**

12   **fresh Mission figs, halved**
        Nonstick vegetable cooking spray, *Pam*®
4   **ounces Brie cheese, cut into wedges**
        Baguette-style French bread slices, toasted

1. Set up grill for direct cooking over medium heat (see page 15). Oil grate when ready to start cooking. Meanwhile, for Orange-Honey Drizzle, in a small saucepan, combine honey, orange juice concentrate, and herbes de Provence. Simmer over medium heat for 2 minutes. Set aside.

2. Lightly spray cut sides of figs with cooking spray. Place figs, cut sides down, on hot, oiled grill. Cook for 2 to 4 minutes or until figs are tender and marked. Serve fig halves and Brie cheese on bread slices. Top with Orange-Honey Drizzle.

INDOOR METHOD:
Prepare Orange-Honey Drizzle as directed. Preheat broiler; spray a baking sheet with nonstick cooking spray. Broil cut figs on prepared baking sheet 6 to 8 inches from heat for 1 to 2 minutes per side. Serve as directed.

Ember-Roasted Apples with Chocolate-Port Sauce

Prep 20 minutes
Roast 10 minutes
Makes 4 servings

If you're looking for a fall dessert that works year-round, you've found it! Tart green apples are stuffed with buttery caramel, seasoned with pumpkin pie spice and sprinkled with spiced rum. Roast them right on the coals to soften the apple's skin and make the caramel melt on your tongue.

4	Granny Smith apples
2	tablespoons butter
2	teaspoons pumpkin pie spice, *McCormick®*

FOR CHOCOLATE-PORT SAUCE:

¼	cup port wine
1	recipe Champion Chocolate Sauce (see page 199)
	Vanilla ice cream, *Häagen-Dazs®*

1. Set up charcoal grill for direct cooking; let burn until charcoal has ashed over. Meanwhile, core apples, leaving the bottoms intact; set aside. In a small bowl, combine butter and pie spice. Divide mixture among centers of apples. Double-wrap each apple with aluminum foil. Set aside.

2. For Chocolate-Port Sauce, in a small saucepan over medium heat, simmer port until reduced by half. Stir into warm Champion Chocolate Sauce. Set aside.

3. Nestle foil-wrapped apples directly into the ashed-over charcoal. Roast for 10 to 12 minutes or until apples are tender, rotating frequently. Carefully unwrap apples; place an apple in each of 4 dessert dishes. Serve warm with ice cream. Drizzle ice cream with Chocolate-Port Sauce.

INDOOR METHOD:
Preheat oven to 375 degrees F. Prepare Chocolate-Port Sauce and apples as directed, but do not wrap apples in aluminum foil. Butter a baking dish. Place apples in baking dish and bake in oven for 30 minutes. Serve as directed.

Tropical Fruit Kabobs with Key Lime-Yogurt Sauce

Prep 20 minutes
Grill 4 minutes
Makes 4 servings

8	large fresh strawberries
1	barely ripe red banana, cut into 1-inch pieces
4	kiwi, peeled and halved
2	cups cut fresh pineapple, cut into 1-inch pieces, *Ready Pac®*
2	cups cut mango, cut into wedges or 1-inch cubes, *Ready Pac®*

FOR KEY LIME-YOGURT SAUCE:

1	cup low-fat vanilla yogurt, *Dannon®*
2	tablespoons key lime juice, *Nellie & Joe's®*
2	teaspoons honey, *SueBee®*
	Pinch cayenne pepper, *McCormick®*
	Nonstick vegetable cooking spray, *Pam®*

1. Soak four 12-inch wooden skewers in water for at least 1 hour. Set up grill for direct cooking over medium heat (see page 15). Oil grate when ready to start cooking.

2. Drain skewers. Alternately thread fruit on skewers. For Key Lime-Yogurt Sauce, in a small bowl, combine yogurt, lime juice, honey, and cayenne. Cover with plastic wrap and store in refrigerator until ready to use.

3. Lightly spray skewers with cooking spray. Place on hot, oiled grill. Cook for 2 to 3 minutes per side or until fruit is warm and soft. Serve immediately with Key Lime-Yogurt Sauce.

INDOOR METHOD:
Preheat broiler. Prepare skewers and Key Lime-Yogurt Sauce as directed. Place skewers on a foil-lined baking sheet or boiler pan. Broil 6 to 8 inches from heat source for 2 to 3 minutes per side or until fruit is warm and soft.

Parties

The word "party" has always been a magic word in my house. Growing up, Saturday night was Party Night. Aunt Betty and Grandpa Al would put our favorite music on the record player and pile the charcoal briquettes on our rickety old grill while my sister Cindy and I helped Grandma Lorraine pat the hamburgers into perfect circles and ice the cake with thick, fluffy frosting. The years went by and backyard barbecues became fish fries at the lake, then Sunday tailgates, then red wine and ribs on my very own apartment deck. The menu changed, but the magic remained.

Any excuse is a reason to gather around the grill—the big game, a birthday, or simply the weekend. This chapter is filled with six party ideas that will make any occasion festive, whether you're marking a milestone or just celebrating a sunny day. Easy-to-make menus are paired with creative tablescapes. A party is one of life's simple pleasures and needs only two things—food and friends. Add a hot grill and a cool cocktail, and you have all the makings of a sensational soiree or a barbecue buffet.

Grillscapes

Branding Iron

Give steaks, chops, chicken breasts, and fish a touch of pizzazz and panache with a personalized branding iron. I had mine tailor-made with my initials since that's my signature trademark, but you can customize one for you or your friends that has a name, word, or symbol on it.

If you're looking for a trendy yet unusual party favor to hand out to guests after your greatest grilling gathering, customized branding irons are a surefire way to score you instant popularity points. Look online for companies that create these tools.

Menu

Buffalo Baby Back Ribs, page 76

Tuscan Veggie Packets, page 24

BV Coastal Estates Merlot

White Cream Cupcakes, right

Biker Bash

When you're in the mood for something a little glitzy and a lot of fun, a biker bash buffet is the way to go. Park a gleaming Harley® deckside, parkside, or lakeside to set the tone, toss the ribs on the grill, and pour the wine. It's a unique way to liven up any outdoor group gathering—whether it's an afternoon get-together, birthday, anniversary, or just a way to treat Dad to a Father's Day fantasy.

Playful accents: Let the games begin with tic-tac-toe boards, poker chips, playing cards, chess pieces, checkers, and other fun game pieces. Bowls filled with dice and packs of unusual playing cards make easy take-away gifts for guests.

Place setting: Chic toile plates pair with polka dot bowls, square black chargers, black-handled silverware, and fanned napkins to make a sophisticated place setting. To make quick playing card place cards, glue a row of three dice to the front and back of a playing card and stand one at each plate. Write each guest's name on the top with a black marker and you're good to go.

Tablescape: Sleek black and white glistens with touches of chrome—on silver trays, silverware, and the pedestaled glass cupcake stand. Cover the table with a silvery silk remnant, adding extra sparkle with curvy glass candelabras bearing tapered black candles. Slender black-stemmed goblets echo the look.

Food and drink: For Creamy Cupcakes, ice store-bought cupcakes with canned frosting given a flavor boost with almond extract, then decorate with black and white candles. Treat the table to splashes of rev-it-up red with glasses of BV Coastal Estates Merlot and baby back ribs (remember, no drinking and driving).

Menu

BBQ Brisket with Guinness® Mop Sauce, page 127

Asparagus with Spicy Mustard Dipping Sauce, page 27

Solaris Napa Valley Zinfandel

Ember-Roasted Apples with Chocolate-Port Sauce, page 216

Fete in the Forest

A spring birthday, the first day of autumn, or just a celebration over the refreshing nip in the air are glorious occasions for a fall feast. A hearty supper of barbecue brisket with a savory sweet Guinness® sauce, crusty rolls, nutty asparagus, a fruity red wine, and chocolatey ember-roasted apples bring fall's harvest to a textured table that comes alive with greens, golds, and touches of reds.

Place setting: Ribbed green glass plates layer texture on texture stacked on a black fluted charger and topped with a wooden bowl; inside, a silk butterfly alights on a spruce green napkin that makes an easel for a computer-printed place card. Just glue a white vellum card diagonally across a green one and prop in place.

Tablescape: Mother Nature provides the backdrop—and the inspiration—with a golden leaf-sprigged tablecovering and straw-wrapped candelabras entwined with woodsy greenery, moss, and fern-colored taper candles. Mossy twig bird's nests cradle votives in glass holders.

Menu

Lemon-Herb Grill-Roasted Chicken, page 147

Smoked Tomato Salad, page 24

Jose Cuervo® Golden Margaritas

Lemon-Blueberry Layer Cake, right

Picnic by the Pond

A dappled blue-green palette radiates tranquility, whether you're dining by the water or on your own patio. Glittering glass, verdant greenery, and a summery menu of lemon-herb chicken, smoked tomato salad, and lemon-blueberry cake make it a stylish setting for any bright spring or summer occasion—such as a Mother's Day luncheon, a May Day celebration, or a early-evening summer supper.

Tablescape: Aquatic colors come together in a madras plaid tablecloth, accented with translucent green votive holders and blue martini glasses. Celadon leaf plates, lotus-shaped bowls, and pebble place mats underscore the retreat feel and make a natural companion to a garden-grown meal.

Lily pad place card: A circle of paper, green felt, and a faux lily make a pretty place card.

Lemon-Blueberry Layer Cake: Dessert's a breeze when you start with two round store-bought cakes sliced in half horizontally and stacked with mounds of creamy vanilla frosting or whipped topping between each layer and on top. For homemade flavor, add a few drops of lemon extract to the frosting or whipped topping and garnish with blueberries, lemon slices, and fresh mint.

Floral focal points: Fold swanlike lilies and trailing sprigs of greenery into shallow cylindrical glass vases for an enchanting centerpiece. Flank with tall slender vases filled with pondside plants, such as hostas, wood ferns, and primrose, to lushly integrate the table and setting.

Menu

Varsity Dogs, page 52

Potato Salad with Bacon Ranch Dressing, page 20

Touchdown Punch, right

Chocolate-Coconut Cake, right

Toast to Tailgating

Easy to make and easy to eat—that's the ticket for this peppy tailgate. Your school colors cue the table, so grab your megaphones and pom-poms and get set to kick off the weekend. The all-star theme works for every sport and every occasion, from game day to birthdays, graduation, or a class reunion. Enjoy all-American food such as dressed-up hot dogs, potato salad, and chocolate cake.

Tablescape: Get the crowd going with grilled Varsity Dogs and dressed-up deli sides served on a green turf mat complete with 50-yard line. (Make your own by cutting yellow and white line markers out of felt and hot-gluing them down the center of a synthetic turf mat.) Tall glass vases make five-minute centerpieces stuffed with pom-poms and home team pennants.

Place setting: Craft store ceramics and school pennants are just the ticket for table decor. Turn a football mug upside down on a matching bowl and stack on a football field plate and a large white charger. Initial pennant place cards cut from felt guide guests to their seats.

Dessert and drink: Here's something to cheer about: a fantastic cake you can make in minutes. To make the Chocolate-Coconut Cake, slice two store-bought unfrosted round chocolate cakes in half horizontally and spread canned chocolate frosting and a generous sprinkling of toasted coconut between each layer and on top. Keep spirits high with Touchdown Punch mixed by the bowlful. Combine 1 can of Hawaiian Punch® with 1 can of apple cider, 1 liter of Fresca®, and 1 liter of cranberry juice. For an adult drink, add a shot of vodka to each glass and top it off with punch.

Menu

**Brilliant Bacon
Burgers, page 178**

Pizza Margherita, page 32

Cream soda or root beer

**Old-Fashioned Chocolate
Sundaes, right**

Rudy's Drive-In Buffet

Turn back the clock to a time when carhops skated dinner to your car window. Cheery checks and down-home diner food turn a retro theme into a nostalgic birthday or anniversary party, a warm weather picnic, or a back-to-school send-off. Put on that old-time rock and roll, bring on the burgers, and dish out the scoops of ice cream for sundaes—now is the time to enjoy a blast from the past!

Tablescape: A '50s plaid tablecloth and napkins are a colorful canvas for Brilliant Bacon Burgers and kettle chips served on red carhop trays; white plastic plates (find these plates online at www.worldwidefred.com), plastic utensils, red root beer mugs, and drive-in menus slipped in plastic holders round out the diner decor.

Old-Fashioned Chocolate Sundaes: For dessert, dish up a taste of nostalgia. Scoop vanilla ice cream into a vintage sundae dish, drizzle with Champion Chocolate Sauce (see recipe, page 199), and top with crushed sugar cones and maraschino cherries.

Place cards: Pen each guest's name on a red-bordered name tag and stick it on a plastic ketchup bottle to make place cards.

Centerpiece: Red tulips look picnic-perfect arranged in red gingham takeout cartons. Mix in a few thermal jugs filled with white carnations for instant ambience.

Menu

**Grilled Sausage-and-
Summer Vegetable
Pasta, page 63**

Crusty French bread

**Blueberry Dream
Cocktails, right**

**Vanilla Cake with
Blueberry Sauce, right**

Sunny Soiree

If you need an excuse to throw a party, here's a good one: It's spring! Sunny daisies, ripe berries, and cabana stripes mix with a make-it-fast menu of grilled vegetable and sausage pasta, a hit-the-spot blueberry cocktail, and a vanilla cake crowned with blueberries. The classic style is beautifully refined, just right for Easter, Mother's Day, a bridal shower, or a dressy brunch.

Blueberry Dream Cocktails: Blue-stemmed glasses are an elegant showcase for a fun fruitini. Mix Smirnoff® Norsk vodka with a splash of lemonade and drop two or three blueberries in the glass to garnish.

Place cards: Crowned with a ribbon and a daisy, a place card box ties it all together.

Tablescape: Gilt-edged blue filigree china and an awning stripe tablecloth set the tone for a menu that's casually elegant. Bunch daisies in a footed cobalt vase for a simple centerpiece, repeating the theme in water glasses at each plate.

Vanilla Cake with Blueberry Sauce: Skip the baking and sandwich two store-bought unfrosted round cakes together with plenty of creamy vanilla frosting and swirls of frosting on the tops and sides. Garnish with blueberries on top and around the base. Serve with a gravy boat of canned blueberry pie filling as a sauce on the side.

Index

Free

Lifestyle web magazine subscription

Just visit
www.semihomemade.com
today to subscribe!

Sign yourself and your friends and family up to the semi-homemaker's club today!

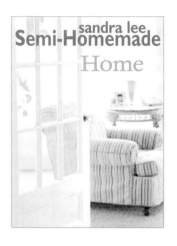

Each online issue is filled with fast, easy how-to projects, simple lifestyle solutions, and an abundance of helpful hints and terrific tips. It's the complete go-to magazine for busy people on-the-move.

tables & settings	fashion & beauty	ideas	home & garden	fabulous florals
super suppers	perfect parties		great gatherings	decadent desserts
gifts & giving	details	wines & music	fun favors	semi-homemaker's club